Education and Social Mobility

IOEPress Trentham Books

Education and Social Mobility
Dreams of success

Kate Hoskins and Bernard Barker

A Trentham Book
Institute of Education Press

First published in 2014 by the Institute of Education, University of London,
20 Bedford Way, London WC1H 0AL

ioepress.co.uk

British Library Cataloguing in Publication Data:
A catalogue record for this publication is available from the British Library

ISBNs
978-1-85856-613-9 (paperback)
978-1-85856-614-6 (PDF eBook)
978-1-85856-615-3 (ePub eBook)
978-1-85856-616-0 (Kindle eBook)

Typeset by Quadrant Infotech (India) Pvt Ltd
Printed by CPI Group (UK) Ltd, Croydon, CR0 4YY

Cover image by Julia Dawson

Contents

List of figures and tables

List of abbreviations

A level	Advanced level
BCS	British Cohort Study
BERA	British Educational Research Association
BHPS	British Household Panel Survey
BTEC	Business and Technology Education Council vocational qualification
DCMS	Department for Culture, Media and Sport
DfE	Department for Education
EBC	English Baccalaureate Certificate
FE	Further education
FSM	Free school meals
GCSE	General Certificate of Secondary Education
GDP	Gross domestic product
HMG	Her Majesty's Government
KS2	Key Stage 2
KS3	Key Stage 3
KS4	Key Stage 4
KS5	Key Stage 5
LCC	London County Council
MDS	Millennium Cohort Study
NCDS	National Child Development Study
NEP	National Equality Panel
Ofsted	Office for Standards in Education, Children's Services and Skills
PFAP	Panel on Fair Access to the Professions

PhD	Doctor of Philosophy
PLASC	Pupil Level Annual School Census
RAT	Rational action theory
RE	Religious education
SEN	Special educational needs
SATs	Standard Assessment Tasks
UK	United Kingdom
US	United States

For the next generation: Zachary, Conrad and Marcel

Acknowledgements

We were both educated in London comprehensive schools and believe in the reciprocal connection between knowledge and power. As teachers, we insist on the link between education and democracy, and between learning and self-government, and share without reservation Aneurin Bevan's belief that:

> education is primarily concerned with the ordinary person, and not with the exceptional person. The ordinary person is asked to decide issues of far greater gravity than any exceptional person in the past... When I complain about our secondary schools imitating the public schools it is because they have a different task to perform ... In order to be on terms of equality with the product of public schools they must be trained differently ... These boys and girls are to be asked to wield the royal sceptre; we must therefore give them the souls of kings and queens.
>
> (Bevan, quoted in Foot 1962: fn p. 140)

But our experience has made us sceptical about other claims made for education, especially the proposition that state schools should aim for every child to achieve academic success and climb the ladder of opportunity. Since the turn of the century politicians have begun to turn Bevan on his head, and to demand that comprehensives *should* imitate public schools, *should* emulate elite values, and *should* expect to close the gap between less and more advantaged children. Our mistrust of these ideas is based on our own journeys through education and is the foundation for this enquiry into our respondents' dreams of success and their chances of upward social mobility.

We are indebted, therefore, to our professional colleagues, friends and families who have informed our sense of the aims and purposes of education, and who have considered and debated our interpretation of the relationship between schools and society. David Kennedy, Dave Allman and Jonathan Culpin have played important roles in shaping the research, while Jane Martin and Diane Reay have contributed generously by reading and commenting on our manuscript. We are especially grateful to Gillian Klein for her care and skill in nursing our project from its inception and her infinite pains to shepherd us through to publication.

Our principal obligation is to the 88 students at South Park and Felix Holt academies who participated eagerly in the research interviews and described vividly the details of their lives, families and dreams. Their voices and perceptions may be heard throughout the book and we hope that our account captures something of their youthful optimism and idealism.

We are also grateful to friends and colleagues at the Institute of Education (for providing Bernard with a visiting fellowship) and the University of Roehampton (for encouraging and supporting Kate's research). As ever, Ann and Damien have been our main support, tolerating long spells at the keyboard and endless speculation about whether the gap really can be closed.

We are much obliged to the *Financial Times* for permitting us to reproduce two figures from their analysis of differential school performance, and to The Equality Trust for approving our use of a figure from Richard Wilkinson and Kate Pickett's *The Spirit Level*.

About the authors

Kate Hoskins is senior lecturer and programme convener for the MA in Social Research Methods at the University of Roehampton.

Kate completed her undergraduate degree in Education Studies at London Metropolitan University, followed by a Master's degree and PhD at King's College London. She taught modules on the MSc in Youth Studies at Birkbeck while she was studying.

Kate joined Roehampton in 2010 as a full-time lecturer and has delivered a range of modules on the BA Education programme, including on education policy, youth identities and research methods. She became programme convener for the MA in Social Research Methods in January 2013 and teaches several modules on the programme.

Her academic publications are concerned with issues of identity and inequalities in further and higher education. In her book *Women and Success: Professors in the UK academy* (Trentham Books, 2012) she used life history interviews with 20 female professors to reveal the persisting inequality facing senior women working in higher education. She is working on a small project, funded by the Centre for Educational Research in Equalities, Policy and Pedagogy, exploring youth transitions and youth education policies to show how young people's pathways are shaped by their identities.

Bernard Barker is emeritus professor of educational leadership and management at the School of Education, University of Leicester, and visiting fellow at the Institute of Education, University of London (IOE).

He was educated at Eltham Green, a prototype LCC comprehensive that inspired his passionate commitment to all-ability schools, and won an open exhibition in history at Gonville and Caius College, Cambridge. He progressed to York University where he researched the Labour movement in the years immediately before and after the First World War.

Between 1971 and 1999 he taught at schools in Hertfordshire, Cambridgeshire and Leicester, including 17 years as the principal of Stanground College, a large community comprehensive in Peterborough. His book *Rescuing the Comprehensive Experience* (Open University Press, 1986) reaffirmed the importance of comprehensive education in the threatening environment of the Thatcher years.

He joined the School of Education at Leicester in 1996 to teach the secondary history Postgraduate Certificate of Education (PGCE), became a facilitator with the National College's Leadership Programme for Serving Heads (LPSH) and provided training and consultancy for schools throughout the UK. He has tutored Leicester MSc and EdD degrees around the world. He was appointed to a personal chair in 2006 and became director of postgraduate research studies for the School of Education.

His recent academic publications include over twenty peer-reviewed journal articles and the books *Transforming Schools: Illusion or reality* (Trentham, 2005), *The Pendulum Swings: Transforming school reform* (Trentham, 2010), and *Human Resource Management in Education: Contexts, themes and impact*, with Justine Mercer and Richard Bird (Routledge, 2010).

Chapter 1

Introduction

Social mobility has become an important policy theme, pursued with increasing vigour by New Labour and Coalition governments for more than a decade. Numerous official documents[1] have argued that upward mobility has stalled in recent years and have urged that action be taken to ensure fair access to a good education and better jobs. Ministers have become determined to 'open doors' and 'unleash potential' so that large numbers of people are enabled to climb the ladder of opportunity, no matter how disadvantaged their origins. These ministers wish to create a demonstrably more meritocratic society in which inequality is based on achievement rather than heredity (Flannery and Marcus, 2012).

Policy-makers are passionately committed to an individualist, emancipatory conception of education, although official reports have sometimes admitted that disadvantage can slow the emergence of an open, meritocratic society (Aldridge, 2001). Governments have nevertheless rejected sociological perspectives that place education amongst the unequal structures it is supposed to transform, and have consistently denied that schools tend to reproduce the social order rather than to liberate less fortunate students from subordinate positions (Bourdieu and Passeron, 1977). This reluctance to acknowledge or respond to an obvious criticism has weakened government claims that the right kind of education can overcome disadvantage (Gove, 2012; Barker, 2011).

Education and Social Mobility examines Coalition plans (Department for Education [DfE], 2010a; Her Majesty's Government [HMG], 2011) to increase social mobility in England and considers the prospects for their success in light of qualitative interviews with 88 school students, aged between 15 and 19, enrolled at two state secondary schools. We invited these students to reflect on their lives, education and dreams for the future. Their identities are protected by the use of pseudonyms for the two academies where the research was carried out (South Park; Felix Holt) and for the young people themselves (listed in Appendices 1 and 2). We concentrate on proposals to reform education for the 15–19 age group because this is where the Coalition is boldest and most convinced that the entrenched problems associated with improving social mobility can be resolved (DfE, 2010a). We ask whether the Coalition government's education reforms can overcome the main obstacles to increased social mobility in England and investigate essential flaws that compromise the validity and usefulness of official models of social change and mobility.

Anna and Elijah

In modern conditions of turbulence, competition and intense status anxiety, social mobility concerns have acquired a new salience because they highlight the extent to which the prevailing social order provides (or fails to provide) a fair reward for merit, effort and usefulness. Increasing evidence of apparent injustice touches recession-damaged nerves and provokes questions about the legitimacy of a social regime where silver spoons and adversity seem to be inherited rather than deserved, and in which schools appear to magnify rather than reduce the consequences of family background (Crozier *et al.*, 2008).

Consider, for example, the stories of Anna and Elijah, 16-year-old General Certificate of Secondary Education (GCSE) students at South Park. Both gave perceptive, thoughtful accounts of their families, school education and future prospects, and warmly praised their teachers. Their disparate narratives illustrate the intricate, uncertain links between education and social mobility, and suggest the pitfalls that hinder our understanding of the ways in which background variables impinge on personal disposition and ability.

Elijah is a gifted student, predicted to achieve A* GCSE grades in all his subjects. His father is a professor at a world-class university while his mother is a leading cancer researcher. They are prepared to 'spend what it takes for me to do well' and have paid for private tuition to provide extra challenge in mathematics and to enable Elijah to take GCSE German two years early. Elijah is keenly interested in world affairs, watches the news and reads newspapers, and acknowledges the influence of books like Orwell's *1984* and *The Ragged-Trousered Philanthropists*. He has travelled around the world with his parents, including a spell in Sydney 'while my dad was doing consultancy in structural engineering'. Elijah is ambitious and strives 'to be the best at what I do'. He is considering economics, international relations or aeronautical engineering as career options, and envisages that people like him can become engineers and then 'spin off into a high-tech manufacturing company'. He expects to transfer to one of the country's top sixth form colleges to study Advanced (A) level mathematics, further mathematics, physics, economics and history.

Anna comes from a large, 'quite disadvantaged' family and is predicted to achieve C or D grades at GCSE. She says that 'we don't get as much money as others' and that this has affected her ability to go on school trips and to buy art materials for use at home. This is not a serious problem, because

2

the school art room is well equipped, 'but it would be nice to have it at home, your own'. Anna's parents fully support her education, however, and 'talk to me as much as possible, making sure I understand everything'. She is determined to get her target grades and is motivated by lessons 'without loads of writing'. She has applied to the regional college for a level 2 childcare course, much influenced by a successful experience at a local nursery and by her sisters who 'explained what you learn'. Her parents think 'childcare is a good option for me because I'm good with my younger brothers and sisters. I've helped a lot with children at home.' She's happy with her way of life and is confident that in the future 'I'll be just fine living like my parents'.

These accounts capture stark contrasts between the two respondents and their very different backgrounds, but they are not extreme or unusual cases. Anna is a capable, average student who was more than able to express wise thoughts and feelings about her family circumstances and future prospects. She is one of the C/D borderline candidates who have attracted extra attention from schools chasing performance targets, and she has responded by working hard towards well-defined goals that will advance her career. A large number of school students across the country will achieve less good results than this. Even so, Anna and Elijah, students at the same highly-rated state comprehensive, are divided by significant differences in family background and income that seem to be reflected in their divergent academic progress and aspirations. Anna is aiming for a further education qualification and a relatively low-income job in childcare, while Elijah is headed towards an elite university and a secure professional career.

At age 16, Anna is amongst those students 'from deprived backgrounds' who 'are less than half as likely to go on to study at university as their peers' (Gove, 2012, unpaged) and already seems set for a lifetime of below-average earnings. Her trajectory through school, and her ready acceptance of the vocational career route recommended by her family, helps explain why only 'one in nine of those with parents from low income backgrounds reach the top income quartile' (HMG, 2011: 5).

Moral purpose

Michael Gove, secretary of state for education, interprets stories like this as evidence of systemic failure in education and asserts that 'access to a quality education is rationed for the poor, the vulnerable and those from minority communities' (Gove, 2011a, unpaged). His indictment is vivid and apparently sincere:

But, tragically, there are all too many children who still don't leave school with these basic accomplishments ... And the greatest tragedy is that poor educational performance is concentrated in our most disadvantaged communities – places like Knowsley in Merseyside, Hull and East Durham. Because of my own background, I am determined to do everything I can to help the poorest children in our country transcend theirs.

(Gove, 2013, unpaged)

Convinced that the 'weaknesses of our system' are blocking social mobility, Gove says he is passionate about improving teaching, raising standards, and 'narrow[ing] the gap in attainment between rich and poor' (DfE, 2010a: 15). He declares that his 'moral purpose in Government is to break the lock which prevents children from our poorest families making it into our best universities and walking into the best jobs' (Gove, 2011a, unpaged).

Gove's moral indignation is admirable but in this case may be misplaced. Anna and Elijah attend South Park, a community school with an enviable local reputation, a good inspection report, and excellent examination results. Both students have unrestricted access to capable teachers and a positive, well-equipped learning environment. A good proportion of South Park students, including Elijah, achieve A* GCSE grades and go on to gain entry to a prestigious local sixth form college. Borderline candidates already receive extra help, especially through a programme of revision classes, while Anna is set to clinch her target grades and secure a place at the regional college.

This ambiguous case exemplifies a much larger national problem and prompts significant questions that policy-makers should ask before surrendering to their passions. How should the egregious performance gap between different groups of students be explained? Should South Park be blamed for 'gaps in achievement between rich and poor' or praised for designing an appropriate, differentiated curriculum for students with dissimilar interests and abilities? Are these 'gaps' the result of weak, possibly misguided teaching, or should they be seen as natural phenomena, the predictable outcome of an unequal society where all kinds of family resources are abundant for some and painfully thin for others? Alternatively, 'the gap' could be an inescapable function of the statistical techniques used to convert examination marks into grades. The desire to reduce the distance between those at the top and bottom of the normal mark distribution curve may be as forlorn as a quest for the secrets of perpetual motion.

Obstacles to social mobility

These issues are difficult to resolve because the barriers to relative social mobility are so poorly understood. Possible obstacles include straightforward impediments like social class, childhood poverty and anti-competitive practices that produce recruitment bias or limit access to the professions, as well as less-quantifiable factors like family capital, attitudes and expectations (Savage, 2000; Aldridge, 2001; Mills, 2008; Jackson, 2009; Panel on Fair Access to the Professions [PFAP], 2009). A dramatic rise in inequality in the United States (US) and Britain since the 1970s is now closely associated with growing social problems as well as reduced opportunity for those on middle and low incomes (Stiglitz, 2012). Epidemiological evidence suggests that 'countries with bigger income differences tend to have much lower social mobility', and that inequality has negative consequences for everyone, but especially for those placed towards the lower end of the income spectrum. Mathematics and literacy scores are markedly worse in more unequal countries while school drop-out rates are higher in the less-equal US states (Wilkinson and Pickett, 2009: 159).

Skills and ability, whether genetically inherited or developed through socialization, play a significant role in shaping life chances. Their precise contribution to individual mobility, however, is not easily determined, mainly because the effects of nature (genetics, DNA) are not easily distinguished from those of nurture. Family culture and parenting styles, for example, have been found to influence learning and also the disposition to learn (Lareau, 2002). The recent discovery that the formation and development of synapses in early childhood has a lasting impact on later capability has further complicated attempts to disentangle the relative effects of inherited and environmental factors. Stimulating families and contexts seem to produce durable, beneficial changes in neuronal function (Smail, 2008).

These influences on individual mobility do not operate in isolation from one another, however, but interact within a wider context that is in a state of perpetual flux, with economic changes creating new opportunities over extended periods of time, as well as eroding seemingly permanent occupational structures. Timing is important for all kinds of success, not least for achieving upward mobility. A list of the 75 richest people in human history, for example, includes fourteen Americans born within nine years of one another in the mid-nineteenth century. Their lives coincided with a major transformation of the US economy that produced unusual opportunity (Gladwell, 2008). Economic changes also help to explain the increase in absolute mobility found in Britain after 1945, when rapid growth and the emerging welfare state produced 'more room at the top' for those born in the 1930s and 1940s (Goldthorpe, 1987).

All this makes it hard to decipher Anna's story. Is she naturally less academically capable than Elijah and therefore well served by the education system (Saunders, 2010)? Alternatively, do state schools operate in ways that disadvantage students who are not traditionally 'academic' (Gove, 2011b)? Does her vocational choice represent a rational assessment of the costs and benefits of higher education from her family's class standpoint, as suggested by rational action theory (RAT)? Unchanging class differentials in educational attainment are believed to reflect 'similarly unchanging relativities as between the costs of education and typical levels and dynamics of family income from class to class' (Goldthorpe, 1996: 493). On the other hand, an unequal distribution of resources may have permeated her family, formed her dispositions and so reduced her academic engagement and effectiveness (Mills, 2008; Atkinson, 2012). She may also be constrained by gendered processes that contribute to social reproduction, although none of our female respondents saw gender as an obstacle to their success (Arnot, 2002; Martin, 2006). Another possibility is that she could be seen as unlucky to be alive during a period when opportunities are much reduced and incomes for care professionals are falling (Gladwell, 2008; Stiglitz, 2012). Until these competing explanations are properly investigated and assessed, worthwhile policy interventions that have the potential to improve educational and career outcomes for less-advantaged students like Anna are likely to prove elusive (HMG, 2011: 6).

Investigating social mobility

Quantitative designs, based on repeated analysis of large-scale national birth cohorts[2], have predominated in social mobility research, and have produced a puzzling portrait of intergenerational variation in occupations and incomes during the post-war period. Different researchers have reported contrasting results. Eleven studies have shown increasing social mobility, thirteen studies have found stability, and four have identified declining mobility (Lambert *et al.*, 2007). Some experts have found little or no change in total mobility rates despite improved educational and career opportunities, while others have reported a trend of slowly increasing mobility for both men and women (Goldthorpe and Mills, 2008; Lambert *et al.*, 2007).

One influential study, often cited by politicians to justify their intervention, claims that intergenerational mobility declined in Britain between the 1958 and 1970 cohorts, and remains low by international standards (Blanden *et al.*, 2002; Blanden *et al.*, 2005a). The finding has proved insecure, however, with a critical review discovering that in both cohorts around 17 per cent of those born to the poorest 25 per cent of families end up in the richest quadrant. Taken at face value, this could mean that 'Britain has a quite staggering level of social mobility' (Gorard, 2008: 323), an inference at sharp variance with the original proposition that mobility is 'low and falling' (Blanden *et al.*, 2005b). This conclusion encourages optimism rather than pessimism and provides support for those who argue that Britain is a relatively open society, where abilities and hard work are more important than social advantage and disadvantage, and that people from all social classes have been able to take advantage of increased educational opportunities (Saunders, 2010; Heath and Payne, 2000).

These acute differences of analysis and interpretation stem in part from the methods adopted. Economists, concerned with the labour market, have concentrated on intergenerational income mobility, while sociologists and politicians have been more interested in movement between social positions as defined within a status hierarchy (Goldthorpe and Jackson, 2007). Longitudinal, quantitative designs have compared fathers' and sons' incomes, so that women, welfare dependants and others missing from the workplace have been omitted. Mobility has been measured, therefore, in terms of individual males, not in relation to families and households, with insufficient attention given to income fluctuations during an employee's working life. Reports of growing mobility may be related to the increased number of observational points used in longitudinal cross-sectional surveys (Lambert *et al.*, 2007).

Collectively these studies have left us uncertain as to whether the available data indicates reasonable progress towards an achievement-based ideal, or whether there is alarming evidence of a reversion to a heredity-based regime that blocks upward mobility, especially for the disadvantaged. The Coalition is convinced that social mobility has stalled and that radical education reforms will enable poor children to compete on level terms with graduates from the great public schools, but there is no unequivocal evidence for either proposition (HMG, 2011). The unresolved puzzle is this: do observed patterns of social mobility constitute an expected phenomenon, entirely consistent with the well-known characteristics of British society, or do they demonstrate the failure of state institutions to provide genuinely equal opportunities that enable children to fulfil their potential through education?

This puzzle seems unlikely to be solved by continued over-reliance on 'statistical studies of social mobility' that 'resemble the observation of a carnival through a keyhole' (Bertaux and Thompson, 1997: 6). The 'keyhole' provides an unsuitable vantage point for an investigation of the complex conditions that assist or constrain students like Anna and Elijah as they progress from school to work, and are unlikely to aid our understanding of the latent family and community processes that shape their chances of success (Bertaux and Thompson, 1997; Devine, 2004). Our interpretive, qualitative study aims, therefore, to illuminate the social processes that facilitate or hinder young people's responses to their educational and career opportunities, rather than to provide a representative statistical account of increased or reduced life chances. We ask the fundamental question: *How far can the Coalition government's education reforms overcome the main perceived obstacles to increased social mobility in England?*

Methodology and methods

We use a qualitative methodology to explore the meanings that respondents 'attach to their environment and relationships' (Williams, 1998: 8). We investigated the respondents' perceptions of their present circumstances and future plans to gain insight into their worlds, through their eyes, and to capture their meanings and understandings of events.

We carried out 30 minute semi-structured paired interviews with 88 student respondents to gather rich, detailed and descriptive accounts of their experiences and expectations. The semi-structured paired interviews provided space for the respondents to discuss relevant issues not raised directly by the interviewer. These highlighted further areas for investigation and contributed to the co-construction of the respondents' stories. We conducted individual, semi-structured interviews, lasting 30–45 minutes, with 15 teachers. The initial coding of the data was guided by Straussian techniques (Strauss and Corbin, 1990; Strauss and Corbin , 1998). We have also drawn on the concepts of habitus and field, and social and cultural capital (Bourdieu, 1977a). This framework provided a theoretically inflected interpretation of some of the complexities in the respondents' experiences. We have also analysed government policy documents and relevant literature.

Sample

Two highly effective schools, newly converted to academy status, with above-average mixed intakes and GCSE results, were chosen for their conformity to policy-makers' expectations for the conditions required to foster social mobility. Both are believed to offer capable and committed students from aspiring families excellent access to good examination grades, good universities, and good opportunities for social mobility.

The respondents at South Park were selected with the assistance of the principal, the principal's personal assistant and the head of year 11. The sample construction was opportunist but also purposive to meet our criteria. All of those interviewed had parental consent for their participation. We experienced some divergence between the intended sample and the actual sample, due to the timetable and attendance on the day. During follow-up interviews we tried to interview those absent from the first round, but without much success.

At South Park (which accommodates 11–16-year-olds), the sample comprised 46 students and was purposively constructed to include 24 students (12 girls, 12 boys) in Group A, all selected from the year 11 cohort (192 students). This group comprised those individuals expected to achieve A* or A grades in all their GCSE subjects, due to be taken within the next 3 to 4 months. Group B comprised 22 students (10 girls, 12 boys), selected from the year 11 cohort. This group comprised individuals intended to represent the remainder of the ability range, with their estimated grades varying from A to E. The sample was designed to capture differences in perception based on the respondents' ability, gender and background influences (South Park sample details are provided in Appendix 1).

At Felix Holt, an 11–18 academy, the head of the sixth form identified the respondents and the sample was constructed in the same way as at South Park, with constraints on the day producing a divergence between the intended and actual samples. We took too little account of vocational courses in our initial design, so we have relied on statements made by the students for precise information about their courses and examinations. At both schools the principle was the same: there was one group of very able students and another group representing the rest of the ability range. There was no differentiation by nature of course in the construction of the A and B groups.

At Felix Holt the year 13 sample comprised 42 students, and included 18 students (7 girls, 11 boys) in Group A. In Group B there were 24 (13 female, 11 male) students. The sample was designed to capture differences in perception based on the respondents' ability, gender and background influences (Felix Holt sample details are provided in Appendix 2).

The choice of an 11–16 and an 11–18 school enabled us to draw comparisons and contrasts between different age groups progressing through academic and vocational pathways.

Ethics

This research was carried out in accordance with the British Educational Research Association's (BERA) (2011) ethical guidelines. In the first instance we obtained the respondents' informed consent. The students and teachers were informed of their right to withdraw from the research process at any time, were assured that they did not have to answer any questions they did not wish to, and that their participation would not disadvantage them in any way. They were also assured that data would be held securely and confidentially and that their identity would be protected. Anonymity has been ensured by removing any identifying factors and by the use of pseudonyms for both the schools and the students. The respondents were volunteers who chose to take part in the research process. There was minimal harm or risk facing respondents arising from the research focus. The independence and integrity of the study were made clear to respondents.

South Park

We invited some of the teachers to be interviewed to give us insights into their perceptions of the school and their students. We interviewed seven members of staff at South Park, including the principal, the deputy principal, an assistant principal, two teachers and two pastoral leaders. We asked them to describe the school, the area, the intake and the parents.

The principal described the school as truly comprehensive, with a diverse mix of students encompassing a full range of needs and abilities. The deputy principal affirmed this and talked of a truly comprehensive school that is lovely to work in but that has 'challenging pupils, like any other school'. The assistant principal described the students as lovely and very well behaved. All the staff commented that the intake is diverse but also somewhat polarized, with some very privileged students and others who experience high levels of deprivation, but not many in the middle. One of the teachers explained that amongst the staff 'there is a feeling of a split catchment, but overall a strong intake. The split is socio-economic as much as it is by ability.'

The principal described the local area, history and ethos of the school, and told us that for some families low aspirations persist. The teachers said that parental aspirations and involvement varied, with some parents involved and others disengaged. They told us the school has high aspirations for all of its pupils, including those from traditionally less-engaged families. One of the pastoral leaders said 'we encourage people to dream their dream and do what they want to do'.

Felix Holt

At Felix Holt we interviewed eight members of staff, including one associate head teacher, one middle manager, one Every Child Matters co-ordinator, two teachers, one assistant head, one deputy head of the lower school and one deputy head. Again, we asked them to describe the school, the area, the intake and the parents.

The assistant head explained that the school is an 'all-ability comprehensive with opportunities for all students'. Respondents agreed that the local area is 'lovely', 'nice' and 'safe', and described local people as 'polite', 'kind' and 'family oriented'. One teacher said the intake was 'incredibly white and there is a strong lack of ethnic minorities and religious diversity ... and this limits [students'] outlook on life'. The assistant head and deputy head made similar references to the school's homogeneous intake. The deputy head of the lower school linked the lack of diversity in the intake to many students' 'constrained' aspirations:

> The biggest problem is that we have incredibly talented students who don't know how good they can be ... It's not a diverse area, so students are not worldly-wise ... It worries me that they don't have conversations around the dining table of the wider world and they generally have blinkered views on a lot of world issues.

One of the teachers concurred and told us that at Felix Holt one of the biggest difficulties is that students are limited by:

> a lack of self-belief and self-esteem and this holds them back most. So when you ask about the future or aspirations, they don't think they should dream big, and that's what holds them back from going beyond their parents and what they could achieve themselves ... They don't dream.

Only two members of staff mentioned any difficulties with parents, and these were minor issues that occurred rarely. For example, the assistant head felt frustrated with parents who had 'limited expectations and the challenge is not as high as it should be ... They haven't been shown what dreaming big is.' Teachers were far more likely to describe positive, supportive and reciprocal relationships with the vast majority of parents. The deputy head of the lower school said that in his experience:

> Parents and students share the vision of students wanting to be the best they can be – I've never done a negative parents' evening; they all understand the importance of qualifications and value qualifications very highly.

These shared values provided a supportive and encouraging environment that was very beneficial for the students.

Felix Holt – Family employment history

At Felix Holt we saw an opportunity to gather additional information about workplace destinations. The students were in the final stages of their school careers and vocational trajectories were at the forefront of their minds. We invited them to complete an employment history, specifying occupations held by family members over time. We provided a single sheet of paper and invited students to enter family occupations they could remember, including both sets of grandparents and both parents.

The data concerns three generations of the 42 families represented in the study and is presented in the Felix Holt Family Employment History (Appendix 2). This includes the pseudonym (Column A) and group membership (Column B) for each respondent, the remembered occupation for each grandparent and parent (Columns C–H), the student's own current aspirations (Column I), expected advanced or vocational qualification grades (Column J), and intended academic/vocational track (Column K). Students are listed in alphabetical order within Group A, then within Group B.

We are not, however, seeking to make confident assertions about these students and their social mobility. We aim, rather, to explore perceptions that shape decisions, and to understand how their reflexive accounts bear on their academic and career trajectories. Although incomplete and at times fragmentary, the Family Employment History provides contextual information that helps us understand how families influence individual career choices. We are also concerned to use our data, including its obvious flaws, to illustrate the problematic nature of social mobility research and to suggest the limitations of snapshot data concerned solely with comparing father/son incomes at a fixed point in time.

Theoretical framework

As chapter 2 shows, classic analytical tools used in social class research no longer provide a satisfactory framework for understanding the varied attitudes and behaviour of our students. Although the range of alternative perspectives discussed in chapter 2 provides a more sophisticated set of concepts through which to interpret our students' accounts, the level of explanation provided by these concepts remained very general. We wished to scrutinize the tension in many of our respondents' stories between individual agency, shaped by cultural and familial factors, and the wider impact of economic, social and structural factors. The interplay of the individual with her or his environment, including family, community and school, was revealed by the various assumptions, dilemmas and complexities mentioned by our respondents. The work of Bourdieu (1977a), Reay *et al.* (2005) and Ball *et al.* (2000) provides subtle and complex ideas that assist our analysis of the balance between agency and structure in respondents' lives. We draw on the concepts of habitus and field to deepen our understanding of the reproduction of class inequalities and of the impact of class on prospects for social mobility (Bourdieu, 1977a).

Habitus refers to 'a system of durable, transposable dispositions which functions as the generative basis of structured, objectively unified practices' (Bourdieu 1977a). The term characterizes the recurring patterns of social class, social mobility and class fractions – that is, the beliefs, values, conduct, speech, dress and manners – that are inculcated by everyday experiences within the family, particularly in early childhood. These classed patterns are formed of individual and shared group dispositions. The dispositions (capacities, tendencies, propensities or inclinations) that constitute habitus are acquired through a gradual process of inculcation in early childhood, formed from the family milieu as a complex mix of past and present. The system of dispositions that individuals acquire depends on their family's position in society. Therefore, dispositions produced are also structured in the sense that they reflect the social conditions within which they were acquired.

Bourdieu's (1977a) concept of habitus provides a framework for interpreting the impact of different 'fields' (e.g. families, schools and higher education institutions) on individuals. Habitus is dynamic and interconnected to the field in which it operates. We considered the flow of influence and power between habitus and field as a first step towards understanding how the school might influence an individual's habitus by offering alternative courses of action that move students beyond the '"practical sense" that inclines agents to act and react in specific situations' (Bourdieu, 1993a: 5).

The natural familiarity of the schooling system experienced by some young people stands in stark contrast to the persistent disconnection experienced by many others. These differences are, according to Bourdieu (1977a), related to the alignment and mutuality of habitus and field between an individual and the school, an alignment made possible by the possession of valued dispositions and forms of cultural capital. Educational differences are frequently 'misrecognized' as resulting from 'individual giftedness' rather than from class-based, structural differences. This discounts the fact that the abilities measured by academic criteria often stem not from natural 'gifts' but from 'the greater or lesser affinity between class cultural habits and the demands of the educational system or the criteria which define success within it' (Bourdieu and Passeron, 1977: 22).

We use habitus and field to consider how the respondents are disposed to act in certain ways as a result of their class and gender. We also provide an analysis of the role that social structures play in shaping our respondents' habitus, together with an agentic reading of habitus that examines the extent to which the respondents have space and the capacity to choose and act, albeit within the social and material settings in which they operate. Finally, we draw on habitus as a conceptual tool to consider the impact of social mobility in the respondents' stories. The concept has enabled us to recognize that individuals are not freestanding and that, in the process of pursuing their futures, they are implicitly involved in the structures that constrain them.

Overview of the chapters

We have formulated five statements to define the conditions we expect to find at high-performing schools where expectations and standards are worked on in ways that should eventually produce greater social mobility. The chapters deal with the statements in the following ways:

Chapter 2: Policy-makers, education and social mobility

1. Policy-makers articulate a rigorous conceptual framework for competitive individualism and social mobility.

We review the ways in which education can improve or even transform absolute and relative life chances for individuals and produce a fairer and more meritocratic society. We consider the evolution of UK government policy on education and social mobility since 1990, and ask whether current proposals are based on a valid and realistic appraisal of available data. We also evaluate alternative theories and interpretations of social fluidity and change in the UK, and assess the constraining influences that have been identified.

Chapter 3: Schools and achievement

2. High-performing schools emphasize excellent teaching, high expectations and achievement. Students believe they are 'authors of their own lives' and work hard to reach challenging goals and targets. They are competitive and accept full responsibility for their own relative success or failure.

We examine the quality and purpose of education at South Park and Felix Holt, and investigate the perceptions of students, parents and teachers. Are the schools performing in ways that match government aims? We assess the extent to which students believe the future is in their own hands and work hard to achieve demanding goals. We also consider the extent to which the students are committed to competitive, individualist aims.

Chapter 4: Families and children

3. Family background has less influence than before on student decisions about education and employment. High-performing schools are reducing outcome differences between less-advantaged students and their peers.

We employ the concept of habitus to interpret students' perceptions of the influence of family background. The chapter explores the role of the family in our respondents' growth and the degree to which home experiences have shaped respondents' personal development, as well as their choices of educational and employment pathways. We assess progress towards 'closing the gap' between more and less advantaged students, represented here by members of the A and B groups.

Chapter 5: Aspirations

4. Students aspire to high-status educational and employment opportunities associated with increased chances of relative social mobility. They seek a degree of power and autonomy in their work, and to accumulate economic security and material advantage.

This chapter examines respondents' aspirations for their future careers and family lives. We examine five aspirations that emerge from the interview data and consider them in the context of government social mobility policy and in relation to the concepts of habitus and disposition. To what extent do respondents aspire to happiness, satisfaction, making a difference, status and wealth? We examine a possible mismatch between policy aims and student goals.

Chapter 6: Choosing the future

5. Students have clear, rational understandings of available options and routes through secondary and higher education, training and the workplace. Future choices and outcomes are based on 'horizons for action' that transcend disadvantage and family background.

We review the interview evidence about our participants' choices of academic and career pathways and ask if social mobility policy expectations are justified in light of their thoughts and decisions. We examine whether high-performing schools like South Park and Felix Holt are enabling resilient young people to transcend disadvantage and/or dysfunctional family circumstances.

Chapter 7: Conclusion

The conclusion draws on chapters 2–6 to estimate the extent to which South Park and Felix Holt have succeeded in creating the conditions the government believes necessary for increased social mobility and improved social justice. Have these high-performing schools raised standards and expectations in ways that should produce greater mobility? We assess whether the government's aims and objectives are coherent and realistic, and determine the extent to which these two new academies have succeeded in producing students who strive to advance beyond their parents in terms of academic achievement, status and income.

Notes

[1] Labour strategy documents include Cabinet Office, 2008; PFAP, 2009; and HMG, 2010; Coalition policy proposals have been formulated in DfE, 2010a and HMG, 2011.

[2] Four major studies have provided much of the data used in social mobility analysis: National Child Development Study (NCDS), from 1958; British Cohort Study (BCS), from 1970; British Household Panel Survey (BHPS), from 1991; Millennium Cohort Study (MCS), from 2000.

Chapter 2

Policy-makers, education and social mobility

Introduction

This chapter considers the extent to which education can improve or even transform absolute and relative life chances for individuals and produce a fairer and more meritocratic society. Is the historic expectation that education can become an instrument of social emancipation justified? Or is education itself a status currency, acquired, transmitted and deployed by elite groups to ensure their continued ascendancy? We consider the evolution of UK government policy on education and social mobility since 1990, and ask whether current proposals are based on a valid and realistic appraisal of available data. We also evaluate alternative theories and interpretations of social fluidity and change in the UK, and assess the constraining influences that have been identified. Finally, we ask whether the Coalition government's plans and targets for secondary education are likely to achieve their desired goal.

As Prime Minister, John Major called for a 'classless society' and was confident that prosperity and improved access to higher education would remove traditional class barriers and so open better opportunities for everyone (Childs, 2006). Manufacturing and manual work were in steep decline, class identities seemed to be less and less important, and, as Mr Major himself pointed out, a new economy was emerging, with seven times as many people working in financial services as on farms (Major, 1995; Savage, 2000). Major argued that 'high-class education is at the very core of a classless society' and showcased Conservative measures that had raised the proportion of young people continuing in education after age 16 from 40 per cent in 1979 to 70 per cent in 1995, and had increased participation in higher education, from one in eight to one in three over the same period (Major, 1995, unpaged).

Upbeat commentators claimed that Britain was becoming a meritocratic society, while ordinary people believed more than ever that hard work, effort and talent were effective in securing upward social mobility (Saunders, 1995; Savage, 2000). Conservative and Labour politicians were equally convinced that excellent education would accelerate individual and

---

social transformation, and that it should become a top priority. Policymakers expected rapid progress towards a society driven by talent and effort rather than by birth and inheritance, and rejected academic complaints that class, poverty, race and gender continued to structure life chances and that equal opportunity was compromised by deep-seated inequalities in the labour market (Hodkinson *et al.*, 1996; Jones, 1997; Skeggs, 1997; Vincent *et al.*, 2013). They were confident that students like Anna and Elijah (see chapter 1) were free to pursue their academic and career goals unhindered, and claimed that poverty was no excuse for under-achievement, a position taken up through the school inspection regime (Carvel, 2000).

Social mobility: low and falling

The Laura Spence affair quickly dented bullish assumptions that the expansion of higher education alone would enable students from less-privileged homes to rise to the top. In the year 2000, Spence achieved A* grades in ten GCSE subjects at a comprehensive school in northern England, but was rejected for a place to study medicine at Magdalen College, Oxford. Gordon Brown, as Chancellor of the Exchequer, protested that it was an 'absolute scandal' that she had been turned down. He blamed 'an old establishment interview system' and declared that it was 'time to end the old Britain where what mattered was the privilege you were born to not the potential you were born with' (BBC News, 2000, unpaged).

New Labour suspicions that institutional structures worked against the disadvantaged were inflamed by research suggesting social mobility had fallen for the 1970 birth cohort compared with the 1958 birth cohort. Intergenerational income mobility was said to have declined 'over the last few generations of school leavers' (Blanden *et al.*, 2005a: 13). Blanden and her colleagues sought wide publicity for their findings, asserting that social mobility in Britain was 'low and falling' (2005b: 18) and that 'the expansion in higher education has benefited those from richer backgrounds far more than poorer young people' (2005b: 20). Their data seems to have inspired Ruth Kelly's assertion, as education secretary in 2006, that social mobility 'has declined, and remains low by international standards', and to have informed Tony Blair's promise to make greater social mobility the priority for his third term as Prime Minister (Wintour, 2004, unpaged; Kelly, quoted in Gorard, 2008: 318). Evidence of an apparent decline in mobility galvanized Gordon Brown to adopt a similar stance during his premiership (Gorard, 2008).

New Labour policy-makers viewed 'low and falling' mobility rates as evidence that the labour market was not working properly. Talented people from humble origins, it seemed, were held back by institutional bias and by marked weaknesses in the education system (Blunkett, 2008: 7). Blair insisted that mobility was 'the great force for social equality in dynamic market economies', and his governments promoted social inclusion together with education reforms that would equip young people to compete in the new global economy (Blair, 2002, unpaged). Ministers believed unfairness and social division would be reduced or even disappear as successive generations achieved upward mobility through better opportunities, open to all regardless of background. They anticipated a dynamic, knowledge-based global economy that would generate an increased supply of higher-quality jobs (Cabinet Office, 2008). This was expected to reproduce the conditions prevailing after the Second World War, when an expansion in professional, administrative and technical employment created headroom for a sizable advance in upward mobility (Perkin, 1989; Goldthorpe and Jackson, 2007).

The problem, it seemed, was that birth, not worth, continued to influence life chances in the UK, despite New Labour's determined effort to raise school standards and tackle disadvantage (PFAP, 2009). By age 11, only 37 per cent of children from the poorest fifth of the population reached the government's expected level at Key Stage 2 (KS2), compared with 97 per cent of those from the richest fifth. At GCSE, only 21 per cent of the poorest fifth achieved 5 A*–C grades including English and mathematics, compared with 75 per cent of those from the richest fifth (Goodman and Gregg, 2010). This extraordinary 54 per cent attainment gap indicated that a significant proportion of the population would be left behind, unable to profit from the expected growth in professional jobs that was supposed to create the conditions for a 'great wave of social mobility in the near future' (PFAP, 2009: 5).

New Labour's PFAP documented the disproportionate extent to which high-status jobs were becoming more rather than less socially exclusive over time, the preserve of people from 'an increasingly small part of the social spectrum' (PFAP, 2009: 6). PFAP concluded that talented young people were thwarted in their aspirations by 'silos between further and higher education' and argued for targeted help to give disadvantaged children 'a fair chance to compete to succeed' (PFAP, 2009: 8). Attainment at age 16 is the key to life chances, they argued, so the supply of good schools should be increased to close the attainment gap, especially in disadvantaged areas. The curriculum experience should be enriched, stated the panel, and partnerships should be established between private and state schools (PFAP, 2009).

As Prime Minister, Gordon Brown welcomed PFAP's report. He believed the world economy would double in size in 20 years, producing one billion new jobs for skilled workers. As 'success in school remains one of the most important determinants of future success', Brown declared that all schools should become excellent, designed to enable every student to overcome learning difficulties and disabilities and so to take advantage of the opportunities for social mobility that were opening before their eyes (HMG, 2009: 6).

Moral purpose in government

The Coalition government has followed New Labour in emphasizing the need to reduce inequality and increase social mobility. Education secretary Michael Gove shares his predecessors' concern that disadvantage might impede the efficient operation of the labour market and argues that 'we still do not do enough to extend the liberating power of a great education to the poorest' (Gove, 2011a, unpaged). Private schools, he argues, are too dominant in a 'profoundly unequal society' (Gove, 2012, unpaged). His 'moral purpose' is to remove the barriers that prevent poor children from climbing to the top (DfE, 2010a: 15; Gove, 2011a, unpaged). The Coalition's main priority is, therefore, to reduce the differences in attainment between rich and poor. We can all, policy-makers assert, become 'authors of our own life stories' when we are freed from the imposed constraints that hold us back (DfE, 2010a: 6).

The Coalition's emphasis on education as an agent of social mobility, rather than on simply raising school standards, has led policy-makers to recognize long-denied background constraints and even to acknowledge that 'we have one of the most stratified and segregated school systems in the world' (DfE, 2010b: 1). *Opening Doors, Breaking Barriers* (HMG, 2011) documents the extent to which attainment and life chances are strongly influenced by gender, disability, race and social class. Private schools educate only 7 per cent of the nation's children but provide 70 per cent of high court judges and over half of the membership of other leading professions. Students at independent schools are three times more likely than those at state schools to obtain three A grades at A level.

A fifth of the school population receives free school meals (FSM) but only one in 100 of these disadvantaged students secures admission to Oxford or Cambridge University. Only 25 per cent of boys from working-class backgrounds secure professional or managerial jobs. The persistent, stable attainment gap between FSM candidates and all other pupils suggests that little progress has been made in reducing inequality (Table 2.1, Deputy Prime Minister [DPM], 2011).

Table 2.1: Percentage of children achieving A*–C in English and mathematics at GCSE, by FSM eligibility

Year	2007–08	2008–09	2009–10	2010–11
% of FSM-eligible pupils achieving A–C in English and maths*	24.4	27.1	31.8	35.1
% of all other pupils achieving A–C in English and maths*	52.4	54.8	59.3	62.5
Gap (in percentage points)	28.0	27.6	27.6	27.4

This evidence is consistent with, and to some extent drawn from, research and reports published during the New Labour period. PFAP (2009) provided detailed evidence that those from privileged and privately educated backgrounds are disproportionately represented in the leading professions. The National Equality Panel (NEP) (2010: 1) drew attention to the 'deep seated and systematic differences' in economic outcomes between social groups, and noted that inequalities in earnings and income were high in Britain compared with other industrialized countries and compared with thirty years ago. The top ten per cent of households, for example, have wealth above £853,000, while the bottom ten per cent have less than £8,800. There are marked inequalities within the spectrum as well as between top and bottom, with the top ten per cent owning more than four times as much wealth as those in the middle. Social background was found to have a marked impact on examination results and subsequent success, with parental education and occupation proving a highly significant influence on children's progress.

The Coalition regards the persistent and apparently endemic attainment gaps between the private and state sectors, and between FSM recipients and their classmates, as evidence that most maintained schools do not lessen the differences between children. Unequal educational and career outcomes prove, policy-makers say, that the system is not working for poor and disadvantaged children, and justify urgent, radical reforms to raise attainment so that more young people, especially those from disadvantaged backgrounds, arrive at age 16 in the 'best possible position' to advance their learning and future careers (HMG, 2011: 44). The declared policy goal is for 'all schools to provide an education which matches the best in the independent sector', so that everyone benefits from better educational and career opportunities (DfE, 2010b; HMG, 2011: 38).

Competitive individualism

This approach is based on long-established assumptions about the relationship between education and social change. Robert Owen (1969), an early-nineteenth-century reformer and one of the founders of the cooperative movement, was among the first to recognize the role that education could play in social improvement. He argued that governments were able to give any character to any community, and that a proper system of education would lead to natural social harmony. He told a gathering of supporters 'A whole community can become a new people, have their minds born again, and be regenerated from the errors and corruptions which ... have hitherto everywhere prevailed' (*New Harmony Gazette*, 1826, quoted in Harrison, 2010: 145).

This conviction was widely shared through the nineteenth and early twentieth centuries, with large numbers of 'the rank and file of the working class world' coming to believe that education was an instrument of social emancipation that would enable them to transform themselves and the wider society (Tawney, 1924: 7). Samuel Smiles, Scottish reformer and author, became a celebrity with his book *Self-Help* (1860), published at the height of the mid-century economic boom. This work popularized the idea that individual character, determination and hard work were the essential ingredients of personal and social progress, and Smiles documented countless examples of famous men who sprang 'from the ranks of the industrial classes' to achieve distinction in various walks of life (1860: 24). He insisted that happiness and well-being are secured not by institutions but by the spirit of self-help that is 'the root of all genuine growth in the individual' and constitutes 'the true source of national vigour and strength'. For Smiles, progress is 'the sum of individual industry, energy, and uprightness'. We should not alter the laws but help and stimulate people to 'elevate and improve themselves by their own free and independent action' (1860: 1–2).

Smiles's assertion that determination and hard work are the essential sources of achievement and social mobility has become folk wisdom, with teachers telling pupils routinely that hard work will be rewarded with a better job. His individualist, competitive conception of social progress also informs the widespread belief that education leads to valuable qualifications, increased social and occupational mobility, and higher status. Aware of themselves and their own circumstances but often with little knowledge of the lives of their parents and grandparents, people seldom reflect on the wider society to which they belong (Wright Mills, 1970). As a result, many assume that they are authors of their own lives, free to choose futures, homes and consumer goods that embody their personal aspirations. Individualism and self-improvement are deeply ingrained in western culture and may be found in many contexts, from school classrooms to religious teaching and the self-help business literature ubiquitous at airport bookshops. The recent rise and spread of a culture of individualism and an economics of individualization has strong historical antecedents, therefore, and is grounded in long-held views of the world (Ball *et al.,* 2000; Savage, 2000).

These popular attitudes help to explain the relatively swift adoption after 1979 of the neo-liberal idea that human well-being is best encouraged by liberating individual enterprise within a framework of property rights and global free trade. The supply-side reforms introduced during the 1980s and 1990s, and the shift from welfarist to post-welfarist values in the management of public services, became mainstream with surprising speed, despite an initial period of industrial resistance, strife and protest (Gewirtz and Ball, 2000). After Thatcher[1], politicians were determined to sustain, and where necessary create, competitive markets that would produce high-quality goods and services with maximum efficiency. Public services, including hospitals and schools, were removed from the supposedly dead hand of local government and were expected to compete locally for patients and students (Harvey, 2005).

Ordinary people, especially the 'idle' and unproductive, were increasingly viewed as an obstacle to economic efficiency and progress. Government agencies aimed, therefore, to reform, educate and align human resources to achieve economic goals. Disadvantaged and dysfunctional families were encouraged to adopt the middle-class values and attitudes associated with success and mobility (Gewirtz, 2001). Citizens were expected to see themselves as individualized and active subjects, defined by their consumer preferences and responsible for their own well-being (Larner, 2000; Archer *et al.,* 2010). Social class was treated as yet another personal trait or lifestyle choice that might compete with someone's generation or choice of designer label as a source of identity. A pervasive, hegemonic neo-liberal discourse has reinforced the 'common sense' individualism through which ordinary people interpret and live in the world (Comaroff and Comaroff, 2001).

Coalition policy

Consequently the Coalition's view of education and social mobility is based on a strongly individualist perspective, and a perceived need to improve the nation's human capital. Radical school reforms are intended to ensure that an excellent education is available to all, with hardworking students enabled to overcome the burden of family and social background, and to achieve a place in society commensurate with their singular character, effort and ability.

The Coalition's overall drive to reduce the budget deficit constrains what can be achieved, however, and spending cuts are unlikely to assist upward mobility. Child benefits are frozen, the Sure Start Maternity Grant will be given for the first child only, higher rates of value added tax have a disproportionate impact on small budgets, and the money spent on maintenance allowances for 600,000 less wealthy post-16 students has been cut from £560 million to £180 million (Channel 4 News, 2010; Paton, 2011). Increased university fees may reduce the extent to which low-income families participate in higher education. Reductions in school budgets may lessen the benefits of the Coalition's Pupil Premium[2], intended to improve educational outcomes for the least advantaged (BBC News, 2012b). Youth unemployment is at a record high, with almost one million school leavers and graduates out of work (Wallop, 2011). Although the reform of the benefit system aims to reduce welfare dependency, these measures offer little practical help for disadvantaged young people (HMG, 2011).

Michael Gove is nonetheless undeterred by the severe economic conditions in which he has to operate. He accepts budget cuts and welfare reductions as facts of life, and has concentrated his attention on radical changes to promote social mobility and reduce inequality. Some observers are uncertain whether education policy has swung in a new direction, and have commented on similarities between Gove's reforms and the policies pursued by New Labour in office. They have drawn attention to the Coalition's taken-for-granted commitment to markets and competition, and the special importance attached to self-managing schools (Lupton, 2011; Hoskins, 2012a).

The new government follows its predecessor in proposing increased school autonomy within a framework of explicit accountability measures (Mansell, 2011). Schools are to shape their own character and ethos, free of central or local bureaucratic control. The academies programme is expanding and open to all schools, not just those in disadvantaged areas. Governors, heads and schools are to be responsible and accountable for their own improvement (DfE, 2010a: 11–12). The Coalition emulates the last government in seeking to raise the quality of teaching. Teacher training is to be reformed to extend the time spent in classrooms and to ensure a strong emphasis on core skills. A national network of Teaching Schools is to be established and the number of National and Local Leaders of Education is to be increased. Teach First is to be expanded (DfE, 2010a: 9).

The proposals also include significant departures from the last government's agenda, however, with new arrangements seeking to promote and accentuate a cluster of 'traditional' academic subjects within a more demanding examination framework. Reforms of the curriculum and examination system aim to establish a 'tighter, more rigorous, model of knowledge which every child should expect to master in core subjects at every key stage' (DfE, 2010a: 10). The National Curriculum will 'become a rigorous benchmark, against which schools can be judged' (DfE, 2010a: 11). The draft National Curriculum includes distinctive changes intended to embody high standards, academic values and traditional approaches (DfE, 2013a). The primary curriculum, for example, is to include more demanding content in fractions, decimals and percentages, while there is to be a stronger focus on scientific knowledge. In English, pupils will be expected to develop a stronger command of the written and spoken word, and in history they will learn about the lives of significant individuals in Britain's past. The secondary curriculum emphasizes detailed subject knowledge, and redresses many areas of traditionalist concern, including, for example, the requirement that historical events should be taught in chronological order. In English, functional skills and formal types of writing are to be given priority over creative writing (DfE, 2013a; DfE, 2013b). Vigorous responses to the consultation on these proposals, concluded in April 2013, indicate that Gove's changes are perceived as radical (SLT, 2013).

Changes to the accountability system further illustrate the Coalition's goals. Examinations are to become much tougher, with the introduction of 'English Baccalaureate' criteria and a new scoring method to reward schools and students who achieve good grades in selected academic subjects. A new 'floor standard' for primary and secondary schools sets an escalating minimum expectation for attainment, while two new measures check on the progress of deprived pupils, and indicate 'how young people do when they leave school' (DfE, 2010a: 13). The announcement and abrupt withdrawal of the English Baccalaureate Certificates (EBCs) has caused some confusion, but the education secretary's determination that examinations should be more rigorous, academic and demanding is unchanged. He plans to reform existing GCSE qualifications to achieve the same objectives (Barker, 2013).

These important departures have created a distinctive, radical policy position. Gove believes passionately that access to an excellent, traditional, academic education, similar to that provided by the best independent schools, will 'liberate every child to become the adult they aspire to be' (DfE, 2010a: 7). He is also confident that state schools, converted into self-governing academies, will thrive within his challenging new curriculum, assessment and accountability regimes, and eventually match the standards of the private sector. The benefits will be transformational, with young people from all backgrounds achieving good grades and appropriate career progression. Gove's distinguishing claim is that a rigorous academic education will improve social mobility for everyone.

There are numerous grounds, however, for questioning whether these radical education reforms can close the gap between the achievements of different groups of students and so promote upward mobility. We consider below the extent to which the government's claims are justified. Are social mobility rates low and falling? Are schools responsible for changing such mobility trends? Can equal access to a top academic education close the gap and improve social mobility?

Social mobility trends

Leading politicians have repeatedly made confident statements about a supposed downward trend in mobility, but their source appears to be just one study, which identified 'a *fall* in the degree of social mobility over recent decades' and claimed that poor children are less likely now to fulfil their potential than were their counterparts in the past (Blanden *et al.*, 2005b: 18, italics in original). This conclusion is drawn from a comparison between members of the NCDS, commenced in 1958, and members of the BCS, commenced in 1970, with each panel comprising over 16,000 individuals. Differences between the cohorts are presented as secure evidence of a worrying downward trend in social mobility, based on large-scale national samples (Blanden *et al.*, 2005a).

The claim is less than secure, however, because only 13 per cent of the NCDS cohort and 12 per cent of the BCS cohort were included in the analysis. Some of this 87/88 per cent reduction in sample size can be explained by attrition, as cohort members dropped out through successive phases of the 1958 and 1970 studies, and by the researchers' decision to include only male children when they compared the income relationship between parents and offspring. Many further cases were excluded simply because the relevant data was missing, with the result that the economically inactive, including the sick and the unemployed, are not represented. Given the high attrition rate, the income relationship difference between those remaining in the 1958 (0.17) and 1970 (0.28) cohorts seems insufficient to justify the claims made and the attention they have received (Gorard, 2008). The original investigators have since found that the supposed fall in mobility has not continued among cohorts born in the mid-1980s onwards (Blanden and Machin, 2008).

There are other reasons for doubting the influential idea that mobility is 'low and falling'. One review has found eleven studies that report an upward trend, compared with four identifying decline, while another striking analysis indicates that 50 per cent of the population has changed class position relative to their fathers (Heath and Payne, 2000; Lambert *et al.,* 2007). Savage (2000) believes that class mobility is the norm, not the exception, for both men and women. Saunders (2010: 46) is scathing about politicians who believe that bright kids from poor backgrounds are held back by an unfair class system, and argues that social mobility is extensive and common. He dismisses the supposed fall in income mobility as 'almost certainly a statistical artefact'.

The 'low and falling' study, like many others with similar designs, is questionable also because its focus on the income relationship between parents and their male offspring does not take account of changes in female paid employment or class identity. The interaction between male and female employment is also neglected, at a time when there has been a huge expansion in the volume and quality of opportunities available for women, including better chances than their fathers of entering the elite service class[3] (Payne and Roberts, 2002). Only 17 per cent of women born between 1950 and 1959 stayed in the same class as their father (Savage, 2000). By 2008, women outnumbered men in most UK medical schools by three to two, prompting fears that men are missing out in a once male-dominated profession (BBC News, 2008). Women's social mobility needs to be understood in terms of their own employment and social class, not in relation to their status as wives, partners or daughters.

John Goldthorpe and his collaborators disagree with both optimists and pessimists and present considerable evidence that the 'low and falling' hypothesis is unconvincing. They say there has been little variation in upward or downward mobility rates, and no significant reduction in class inequalities, since the early years of the twentieth century, despite high rates of economic growth and vast improvements in educational quality and access (Goldthorpe and Jackson, 2007; Goldthorpe and Mills, 2008). Labour market studies that identify falling mobility rates are misleading, they insist, because one-off snapshots of income differences between fathers and sons mask individual career trajectories and obscure changes in underlying employment patterns and job status. Social class provides a better indication of the extent to which differences are transmitted across generations, because class position is systematically related to income level, economic security, earnings stability and long-term prospects (Erikson and Goldthorpe, 2010).

Apparent changes in mobility, they argue, stem from shifts in the size and distribution of social classes, not from increases or reductions in social fluidity over time (Goldthorpe and Mills, 2008). The exceptional demand for professional and managerial personnel since the Second World War, for example, created the conditions for increased absolute social mobility[4], with individuals from lower groups able to secure positions in the elite service class because there was 'more room at the top' (Goldthorpe, 1987; Goldthorpe and Jackson, 2007). But relative mobility rates[5] are unaltered, with the proportion of individuals found in different class positions from those of their families of origin remarkably stable since the 1970s (Goldthorpe and Mills, 2008).

This emphasis on the essential stability of British society over an extended period is consistent with research in the 1990s indicating that the pattern of relative class mobility chances or the degree of equality of opportunity has remained the same through the years covered by the Oxford Mobility Study, the Essex Class Project and the British Social Justice Survey. The authors found class boundaries neither more nor less permeable than in the past. Sectoral shifts towards non-manual work had created more room at the top, but no greater opportunity to get there from less-advantaged social positions. Children of service-class parents were found to be five or six times more likely to obtain service class jobs than those from working-class origins (Marshall *et al.*, 1997). Rates of social fluidity had not increased over many decades and were similar to those found in 11 other countries with market economies (Breen, 1997).

Thus the balance of evidence is not consistent with the idea of a relatively recent downturn in the rates of social mobility. On the contrary, unequal life chances have been a persistent feature of British society over a very long time; mobility rates today resemble those found before the Second World War, and are similar to those found in comparable societies. Absolute mobility has increased at times of economic growth and expansion, but the relative chances of an individual from a less-advantaged background rising to a service class position have remained constant. This is confirmed by a Department of Work and Pensions research report: the authors conclude that trends in social mobility are decidedly resistant to policy interventions, mainly because those in higher social classes seem to have taken greater advantage of the opportunities created by government action, and to have used additional resources to maintain their relative position (Nunn *et al.*, 2007; HMG, 2011).

Social stability?

From some points of view, these indications of social stability, marked by long-term inequality and steady mobility rates, are predictable. The available data seems to confirm expectations for a society with a long history of inequality and may simply reflect the extent to which established elites have been able to benefit from favourable economic conditions. Strategically-positioned managers have enjoyed unusual freedom to manipulate patterns of work and reward within the set of free-market assumptions that has prevailed since the 1980s (Stiglitz, 2012). Hierarchical order is widespread and persistent in modern bureaucratic organizations, including those that seem to be participative and to emphasize teamwork (Diefenbach and Sillince, 2009). Although they do not discuss these possible causes, government publications have acknowledged inequality in the UK and document tangible and persistent social differences in health, education, career trajectory and accumulated wealth (PFAP, 2009; NEP, 2010; HMG, 2011).

Elite formation, stratification and inequality, however 'indefensible'[6] in moral terms, seem to be features of most human societies, and to arise from a mixture of political conflict and economic organization rather than from flaws in education. A recent survey of a vast number of archaeological and anthropological studies suggests that inequality developed during the transition from early hunter-gatherer groups to larger, settled communities. Achievement-based societies became common once agriculture was established. The 'active manipulation of social logic by human agents' seems to have driven the creation of hereditary inequality, although factors such as population growth, intensive agriculture and a benign environment seem to have played a role. People's desires to be thought of and treated as superior have been another powerful motive in the formation of unequal social structures (Flannery and Marcus, 2012: 191). Today's 'rent-seekers', who use their political power to secure a lucrative legislative and regulatory regime, provide a contemporary example of the 'manipulation of social logic' (Stiglitz, 2012).

Stratified, unequal societies, once established, have shown remarkable resilience even in times of turbulence and violent upheaval, often resisting the best efforts of social engineers and revolutionaries. In Hungary, for example, a rich qualitative survey of family histories has shown that overall patterns of social mobility have been broadly similar to those found in western capitalist countries. Life chances for the descendants of all social classes were determined by predictable structural and cultural factors, although the socialist regime favoured skilled industrial workers and farm labourers, and discriminated against professionals and kulaks[7]. There seems to have been little significant change in relative positions within the social hierarchy (Andorka, 1997).

A study of fifty Russian families suggests that even the extreme conditions of the 1917 October Revolution failed to prevent many of the expropriated members of the governing class from reinserting themselves into the Soviet regime. Between 1914 and 1918, almost all the well-to-do and rich were made poor. The Tsarist social order vanished, removing the collective resources that had enabled the former elite to transmit social status.

This trauma does not seem to have prevented significant numbers of children of the old guard from integrating themselves into post-revolutionary society through political activism. It seems that a ruling-class habitus, possibly internalized in childhood as a disposition to organize and direct others, may have contributed to the process (Bertaux, 1997: 250).

If unequal social structures and relative mobility rates have remained more or less stable through war and revolution, we should hardly be surprised at evidence of similar continuity in the UK, particularly when our domestic trends closely resemble those recorded in other Western European countries and the US (Breen, 1997). There has been no successful invasion of the country since 1066, and this has contributed to the stability of British society and institutions over many centuries. Elite families can track their lineage through the 3,000 pages of *Debrett's Peerage & Baronetage* or search for their relatives and antecedents amongst the 500,000 index entries in the *Burke's Peerage & Gentry* database (Debrett, 2010; Mosley, 2003). The distribution of status, wealth and income captured in government statistics[8] has not emerged suddenly but reflects a long history of inequality that has produced privilege for some and serious disadvantage for others.

Current trends suggest that inequality has grown worse; other indicators, including youth unemployment and increased debt, as poor families struggle with lower incomes, seem to be loaded against upward mobility (Wilkinson and Pickett, 2009; Clifton, 2011). The recent increase in payday loans is a particularly worrying development, reminiscent of the debt servitude and debt slavery that anthropologists have identified as factors in the creation of inequality in earlier periods. Families who receive food and shelter in times of need are in 'a poor position to deny ... claims to luxury items and hereditary privileges' (BBC News, 2013a; Flannery and Marcus, 2012: 79).

This evidence about the origins and durability of unequal social structures does not support the idea that education is the decisive influence on life chances. On the contrary, some scholars believe that educational processes are important in social reproduction, aid the transmission of class advantage, and contribute to social stability (Bourdieu and Passeron, 1977). By the mid-twentieth century in the UK, a hierarchy of status and wealth stretched downwards from expensive public schools, like Eton and St Paul's, to historic endowed grammar schools and relatively new county grammars, before descending towards a miscellaneous base that included technical, secondary modern and prototype comprehensive schools. The hierarchy of schools matched the probability of finding students of appropriate class origins within them, with young people selected and steered towards suitable placements, and teachers seeking a congenial class ambience. Individual agency was compromised by social structures that shaped and limited choice (Vincent, 2001; Power *et al.,* 2003). In the post-1945 period, patterns of housing, transport and suburbanization are thought to have reconstructed and reformulated the class system, and to have helped create the social foundations for the hierarchies of schooling that appear today in examination performance tables (Lowe, 1997; Levačić and Woods, 2002).

Is it possible that these historic patterns of unequal wealth and opportunity, compounded through many generations, have no impact on children's prospects of success? Is social mobility constrained by this long, unfair history, or by perceived flaws in the present generation of school leaders and teachers? Policy-makers do not accept debate on these terms, and deny that inequality and history have any bearing on the problem. They are frustrated that increased public spending and a large-scale expansion of opportunity, particularly at university level, have failed to improve relative mobility chances or break the link between family background and subsequent success at school and work (HMG, 2011). They maintain a deep-seated belief in the power of markets and competition to liberate individual talent, create wealth and improve society, leading them to reject arguments about the complexity and resilience of social structures and networks (Larner, 2000; Harvey, 2005).

Policy-makers' political lives and experience have made them agents of a heroic enterprise that introduces competition where it does not already exist and invites individuals to embark on a 'reflexive project of the self', taking responsibility for their own talents, the risks they face, and the choices they make 'amid a puzzling diversity of options and possibilities' (Giddens, 1991: 3). Michael Gove is passionately convinced that we can all become 'authors of our own life stories' when we are freed from the constraints that bind us (DfE, 2010a: 6). Like Samuel Smiles, he envisages a society transformed by hardworking individuals who seek to improve themselves through their own 'free and independent action' (Smiles, 1860: 2).

This viewpoint leads ministers and policy-makers to fasten onto differences between outstanding and less-successful schools and to emphasize underachievement by students from certain social backgrounds (Gove, 2011a, unpaged). Performance data and inspections are used to identify schools and teachers whose results fall below expectations, and to drive the setting of improvement targets[9] (Mansell, 2011). This methodology has produced consistent evidence that schools and teachers are failing pupils and obstructing social mobility. Table 2.1 (see p. 21), for example, shows the remarkably stable GCSE attainment gap between those who receive FSM and the rest. Disadvantaged children continue to perform relatively badly in public examinations, while private school students are disproportionately represented at Russell Group universities (Gove, 2012). 'Bright' children do not do as well as expected and 'poor' children have become invisible, apparently languishing in overlooked suburbs, market towns and seaside resorts (BBC News, 2013b; Henry, 2013). From an individualist perspective, this is a shocking indictment of our schools, rather than evidence that it is difficult for them to defeat structural inequality. Politicians simply believe that a good education must, inevitably, 'break the lock' on upward mobility (Gove, 2011a, unpaged).

Politicians have used the issue of low and falling, or even stable, mobility rates to reaffirm their faith in the transforming power of education and to insist on further reforms of the school system. The suggestion that escalating state expenditure on education has helped the better-off to consolidate their position, rather than creating opportunities for social advance, has become a potent wake-up call and has proved far more influential than previous scholarly discussion of unequal life chances in the UK. The oft-repeated statement that social mobility has gone backwards now supplies an important rationale for education reform. Social justice, once a rallying point for the political left, has been assimilated as a Coalition policy motif. Every school must be as good as the best so that everyone can succeed (Blanden *et al.*, 2005a; Gove, 2011a).

Alternative perspectives

The dominant discourse on education and social mobility thus combines an individualist worldview with a quantitative methodology that is concerned with individual performance (in terms of examination success) and progression (in terms of mobility). Effectiveness research analyses performance data to identify highly effective schools and their characteristics, while numerous studies (discussed above) have used income differences between parents and their children to calculate relative mobility rates (Sammons *et al.*, 1995). The risk is that the chosen methodology simply confirms its own assumptions. Quantitative surveys dealing with individual school characteristics (to explain performance differences between schools) and income variation between generations (to measure mobility) may unreasonably narrow the field of investigation and exclude other ways of thinking about education and social change, including historical and sociological accounts of why mobility rates have altered so little (Bertaux and Thompson, 1997; Reay, 2006).

This is especially important when there are strong grounds to doubt the individualist assumption that schools are the main determinant of examination results. Webber and Butler (2005) added the UK Mosaic Neighbourhood classification system to the records of the Pupil Level Annual School Census (PLASC) and found that the type of neighbourhood in which a pupil lives is a more reliable predictor of his or her GCSE performance than any other information held about them on the PLASC database.

National performance data also shows a strong correlation between GCSE results and relative wealth. The outcomes shown on Figure 2.1[10] trace the steady improvement in GCSE point scores from left to right as the relative wealth of neighbourhoods improves. The above-mean performance shown for advantaged neighbourhoods in the upper right quadrant of the figure is the mirror image of the below-mean performance shown for disadvantaged neighbourhoods in the bottom left quadrant. Figure 2.1 shows relative performance dispersed across the spectrum of inequality, rather than sharply polarized between disadvantaged FSM/Pupil Premium students and everyone else. The gap that policy-makers are so keen to close may be a statistical illusion, produced by applying the FSM criterion to identify students in need of support. The close, graduated relationship between GCSE performance and relative wealth supports the hypothesis that social structure, however conceptualized, exerts a strong influence on student outcomes and limits what can be achieved by school-level interventions.

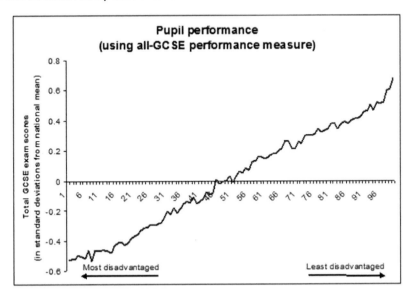

Figure 2.1: Standardized GCSE examination point scores at state schools in 2010, displayed by the relative wealth of neighbourhood (Cook, 2012)

In the same way, a focus on families rather than individuals produces an alternative view of social mobility. Income and occupations cease to be the sole indicators of social position, while family housing, education, culture and inheritance are also taken into account. The role of women in child-raising and as transmitters of family influence becomes apparent, while the family emerges as the principal channel for the transmission of languages, names, land and housing, local social standing and religion, and of social values, aspirations, domestic skills and other taken-for-granted ways of behaving (Thompson, 1997). Life histories and case studies provide opportunities to understand how families may differ in available resources, but also in the extent to which they make effective use of what they have. A relatively poor family may devote funds to advancing a child, while a more prosperous family may have a primary concern with immediate consumption. Dispositions vary and so do the choices people make, even when circumstances constrain possibility (Bertaux and Thompson, 1997).

The evidence that relative wealth is a better predictor of achievement than any school variable raises other questions. If education transforms lives, why have schools found it so difficult to close the attainment gap and improve mobility rates? If students are the designers of their own lives and careers, why do so many follow in the footsteps of parents, siblings and other relatives? Below we review a number of alternative perspectives that challenge ruling assumptions about the relationship between education and social mobility, and furnish resources for a better understanding of why social structures have proved resilient and resistant to change.

Small advantages

Individualist accounts often present upward mobility as the triumph of talent and hard work over adverse circumstances, and direct attention to the unusual personal qualities that enabled the central figure to become outstanding. Malcolm Gladwell's *Outlier* (2008) provides another explanation, arguing that narratives where gifted, determined individuals transcend their circumstances and leap to eminent or wealthy positions in a single generation mask the extent to which eventual success depends on the accumulation of small advantages by families and communities over time. When individuals succeed it is *because* of their personal histories and circumstances, not despite them. He uses the example of his mother Joyce in Jamaica, helped in her pursuit of success by her mixed-race ancestry and local opportunity. He believes that complex interactions of time, place and human culture create propitious conditions in which some people are positioned to exploit chances that were not available to their ancestors.

Dasgupta (2010, unpaged) speculates that even small differences between people can become big cumulatively, with some people trapped in poverty by slight misfortune while others enjoy a progressively better life through equally slight good fortune. The Equality Trust (2012) shows that the advantages accumulated within families are compounded over time, with inherited wealth eventually a significant influence on occupational choice. Dasgupta's (2010) work on socio-ecological pathways has persuaded him that small initial differences in personal or regional histories often divide people and communities into haves and have-nots. The divergent history of three Tuscan towns with radically different patterns of economic and social development, and consequently varied experiences of social mobility, illustrates how divisions can emerge in similar-seeming places (Contini, 1997). The 350 participants interviewed in the 1980s and 1990s for the assisted places[11] evaluation were also divided by minor variations in fortune. Slight differences in examination results were found to produce differing opportunities to translate school achievements into high-status university places (Power *et al.*, 2003).

These insights suggest a continuous adaptive process through which individuals and groups respond to a changing environment, with accumulated advantages and disadvantages enabling or hindering their progress. From this perspective, individual success and failure cease to be the simple outcomes of one person's ability and effort, and appear instead as passing moments in family and community trajectories through time, conditioned by the interplay of agency and structure in ever-changing historical circumstances (Thompson, 1997).

Social class

The concept of an evolving social structure, ordered by class, gender and ethnicity, further calls into question the idea that society is a collection of independent individuals who decide and pursue their own goals. The individualist hypothesis is undermined if people's actions are in reality shaped and constrained by social context, networks and culture in ways that bind families together and transmit their distinguishing characteristics to successive generations. Until at least the late 1970s, there was a ready acceptance that social class and relative disadvantage reduced children's ability to benefit from education and to make progress that matched their ability and effort.

Sociologists of education expected children from manual backgrounds to be placed in low-status schools or in lower streams at comprehensives, and to perform less well than those from non-manual backgrounds (Hargreaves,

1982). A status hierarchy of schools seemed to filter children by their class background. Working-class pupils were less likely to be selected for grammar schools, less likely to do well in public examinations, and much less likely to progress to higher education (Jackson and Marsden, 1986). The lack of social, economic and cultural resources seemed to account for their relative lack of success, and it seemed that 'education cannot compensate for society' (Bernstein, 1970: 344). Other studies claimed that working-class children were disadvantaged by their use of restricted language codes, or pointed to class cultures that resisted the middle-class norms found at many schools (Bernstein, 1971; Sennett and Cobb, 1972).

Since the 1970s, however, many commentators have acknowledged that class identities and solidarity have been eroded by profound changes in the British economy. The skilled working class has reduced from about 70 per cent of the population in the 1950s to little more than 15 per cent by the year 2000 (Bunting, 2009). The organized movements of the working class have been defeated and a majority of the workforce is employed in non-manual occupations (Savage, 2000). The economy is more diverse and complex than before and has generated many new types of employment. The conditions that led to class opposition are said to have been eroded so that class has become 'a less plausible basis for self-recognition and action' (Comaroff and Comaroff, 2001: 11). Class is no longer thought to organize people's attitudes in a consistent way, and class identities are fairly weak. Many scholars have accepted that class is no longer a source of collective identity and that class discourse is disappearing. From a variety of points of view, traditional modes of class analysis are no longer satisfactory (Savage, 2000).

In the classless landscape imagined by John Major, consumer individualism is supposed to replace the fading categories of class, ethnicity and gender so that people become free agents in a meritocracy, rather than classed, 'raced' or gendered members of an unequal society. Social solidarity has been replaced by a 'radically individuated sense of personhood', with people viewed as consumers rather than as producers from a particular community (Comaroff and Comaroff, 2001: 15). There are signs, however, that despite major changes in the economy and workplace, class identities and processes have not disappeared. Instead they are bound up with the processes of individualization and have become powerful through being individualized (Giddens, 1991; Ball *et al.*, 2000; Savage, 2000).

Reflexive life plans may have come to the fore, but class differences continue to be experienced and felt. Between 1983 and 1991, for example, it was consistently found that two-thirds of the population regarded themselves as working class, suggesting that class remains a major anchor for social inequalities. Surveys show that people continue to identify themselves in ways that involve relational comparisons with members of other classes (Savage, 2000). Class categories continue to have a high degree of construct validity because they can be used to show differences across a range of life chances and choices along theoretically expected lines, for example in relation to security of employment and earnings prospects (Goldthorpe and Mills, 2008).

More than 160,000 respondents to the BBC's *Great Class Survey*[12] provided details of their income, the value of their home and savings, their cultural interests and activities, and the number and status of the people they know. The survey reveals a clear gradation in economic, social and cultural capital, ranging from the privileged *Elite* with high levels of all three capitals to the deprived *Precariat* with low resource levels and precarious everyday lives. This suggests that people are no longer divided into sharply-bounded social groups but instead are dispersed in clusters across a spectrum of inequality (BBC Science, 2013). Class now seems to work through the medium of individualized processes (Atkinson, 2012).

Persistent differences in the life chances experienced by dissimilar social groups confirm that the dream of a classless society is far from realization and that class processes continue to shape people's outlooks and prospects. Diane Reay (2006: 303) argues that class remains 'the hereditary curse of English education', the 'zombie' still stalking our schools and classrooms even after more than twenty years of reform designed to improve their effectiveness. She points out that the attainment gap between the classes, like relative social mobility rates, is as great today as it was twenty or even fifty years ago. Working- and middle-class life patterns remain sharply different, with class 'everywhere and nowhere, denied yet continually enacted' (Reay, 2006: 290). Despite reduced levels of class awareness, class differences continue to be important and class itself is 'ever present in people's lived experience' (Savage, 2000; Archer *et al.*, 2010: 10).

Despite considerable overall social fluidity, class background is also closely associated with subsequent occupational destinations. Just 7 per cent of 'high-ability' sons of large business owners and managers were in manual employment by the age of 33, compared with 38 per cent of the 'high-ability' sons of unskilled manual fathers. By contrast, over half of the 'low-ability' sons from professional families join the middle class, compared with 10 per cent of the 'low-ability' sons of unskilled manual workers. Savage concludes that students from middle-class backgrounds are better able to convert their high ability into middle-class jobs than those from the working class, and he believes this superior conversion rate is probably related to the social, cultural and economic resources available to them (Savage, 2000). The absence of such resources could explain why the disadvantaged do less well and why education has failed to improve relative mobility rates (Devine, 2004).

An intuition or a correlation is not the same thing as a cause, however, and uncertainty and debate continue about the obscure or even hidden processes that may lead class or relative wealth to play such a significant role in education. John Goldthorpe's (1996) attempt to explain just one aspect of class stability, that is, the persistence of class differentials in educational attainment, despite a substantial rise in the average level of school achievement, illustrates the complexity of the issues involved. He draws on Boudon's (1974) rational action model to claim that class differentials have persisted despite a big expansion of opportunity because the costs and benefits are viewed from different class perspectives. Young people calculate future life chances on the basis of their perception of their current relative class position, so less-advantaged individuals are more likely to judge that anticipated costs will outweigh anticipated benefits, and choose between different trajectories accordingly.

Class differentials in the uptake of 'ambitious options' are preserved, therefore, because the conditions of advantage or disadvantage in which students assess likely costs and benefits seem little changed (Goldthorpe, 1996: 491). Young people's decisions are rational, he believes, and are based on their understanding of the implications of the resources, opportunities and constraints available. This model allows little scope for the influence of cultural assets and 'distinctions' of the type emphasized by Bourdieu (see p. 13) and rejects the idea that class cultures and the normative commitments of specifically working-class communities limit their educational achievements (Scott, 1996).

Gender and social class

Whilst over the last century women have raised their career aspirations and expectations to include a wider range of employment, researchers have also recognized that gendered career choices have persisted, for example the concentration of women in teaching, nursing and other forms of care work (Smulyan, 2004; Witz, 1997). Pring and Walford (1997: 57) have argued that 'throughout British history social class and gender have been major determinants of the quality of schooling children received'. The persistence of feminine career choices has been attributed to 'patterns including institutional or structural barriers, the internalisation of social norms and gender discourses and differences in values and goals that include career choice' (Smulyan, 2004: 226).

Continuing structural barriers that contribute to female disadvantage include 'promotion practices and policies' that create 'definitions of success based on traditionally male life patterns' (Smulyan, 2004: 227), where males tend to have fewer family and/or domestic commitments. The internalization of gendered norms and gender discourses may act to encourage some young women to position themselves as valuing certain characteristics, such as 'a sense of self as helper rather than leader, as warm rather than ambitious, as emotional rather than rational' (Smulyan, 2004: 227). Such positioning makes teaching, nursing and care work obvious choices for many young women.

To bring together the complexity of class and gender analyses, we utilize the theoretical resource of intersectionality. George (2010: 92) argues for the need to carry out research that explores the 'multiple layers and intersectionality' in female lives to account for the complexity of women's lived experiences. Brah and Phoenix describe intersectionality as:

> signifying the complex, irreducible, varied, and variable effects which ensue when multiple axes of differentiation – economic, political, cultural, psychic, subjective and experiential – intersect in historically specific contexts. The concept emphasizes that different dimensions of social life cannot be separated out into discrete and pure strands.
>
> Brah and Phoenix (2004: 75)

This account suggests that identities are complicated, contradictory, culturally imbued, politically and economically inflected, and historically specific. By exploring strands of an individual's identity we consider how they overlap, conflict and merge, creating, at particular historical moments, specifically contextualized intersections. Skeggs (1997: 2) suggests that exploring the intersections between class and gender is useful, because 'the category "woman" is always produced through processes which include class, and classifying produces very real effects which are lived on a daily basis'.

Many scholars draw on these concepts to explain how the intersections of gender and class may constrain aspirations and influence an individual's approach to opportunities that occur.

Ability and culture
RAT seeks to explain why liberal predictions of better life-chances for individuals from different class origins have not been fulfilled, but nevertheless retains an individualist outlook in accounting for their behaviour. People from similar class backgrounds may have similar preferences, but their actions are seen as the results of personal, rational assessments of their circumstances

and prospects (Goldthorpe, 1996: 483). This prompts the question of how rational decisions may differ from those arrived at in other ways (e.g. following a family precedent) and does not ask about the extent to which individuals are autonomous and able to form and implement their own ideas and choices. The agent is treated almost as an observer, placed outside social processes and invited to make decisions about them.

However, a variety of social and cultural processes provide alternative explanations for the decisions made by students from lower-class positions. It seems, for example, that young people from poor backgrounds are set on negative educational trajectories from an early age, certainly before adolescence. Goodman and Gregg (2010)[13] found big differences in cognitive development between children from rich backgrounds and poor at the age of 3, and report that this gap widens by the age of 5. They also identified equally large differences in birth weight, health and parenting styles. Parents' aspirations and attitudes to education varied by socio-economic position, with 81 per cent of the richest mothers hoping their children will go to university, compared with 37 per cent of the poorest mothers. Adverse attitudes to education 'are one of the single most important factors associated with lower educational attainment at age 11' (Goodman and Gregg, 2010: 6).

Gregg and Macmillan (2009) draw on two British birth cohorts (NCDS, 1958; BCS, 1970) to conclude that the strong relationship between family background and a child's educational attainment represents the extent to which adult outcomes mirror an individual's childhood circumstances. Early experiences can have lasting and sometimes irreversible consequences, with 'nutritional insults in childhood' able to harm a person's ability to work in adulthood. These trajectories of disadvantage have a profound impact on individuals and their ability to choose freely between alternatives (Dasgupta, 2010, unpaged).

Cultural capital, transmitted through the family, seems to have a significant cumulative impact on children's socialization and their development as people (Bourdieu, 1977a; Lamont and Lareau, 1988; Thompson, 1997). Social class has been found to create distinctive parenting styles, with middle-class youngsters gaining from 'concerted cultivation' while less well-off families lack the economic and cultural resources to secure equivalent benefits for their children. Differences in 'the cultural logic of childrearing' provide middle-class children with particular advantages but also with the skills needed to negotiate their life paths (Lareau, 2002: 748). Interviews with 28,000 UK students for the *Taking Part* survey commissioned by the Department for Culture, Media and Sport (DCMS), confirm the role of cultural activities in educational attainment, intergenerational mobility and in the reproduction of class. Young people who were encouraged to participate in arts events, sport and reading had greater chances of social mobility. The disposition to take children to cultural events and to encourage them to read, and to participate in the arts, music and sport, is unequally distributed across the social classes, so the less privileged are more likely to miss out (Scherger and Savage, 2010).

The complex interrelationships between these social, cultural and family processes highlight the limitations of rational decision-making models, where people calculate costs and benefits and act in terms of their self-interest. Agents' strategies are often related to wider issues of identity and identification, and the ways in which these are influenced by class fraction, ethnicity and gender. Identity is not a simple individual choice but reaches back into history, family and the community (Henkel, 2005). People are introduced to the deeply held values, beliefs and attitudes of their locality through the language they learn at home and through their social networks (Crozier *et al.*, 2008).

Some investigators have been surprised by how greatly families emerged as a significant component of young people's social and educational lives. Families played a very significant role in career or life planning but were also important in helping the new generation form social perspectives and generate resources for identity formation. Young people's choices seem not to be the result of unfettered free will, but nor are they determined mechanistically by some external force. Instead, decisions stem from perceptions that are rooted in the identity of the young person, formed through the influence of life history, social and cultural background and interactions with significant others. These processes of socialization and identity formation help explain why less-privileged students remove themselves from higher-status choices and trajectories (Ball *et al.*, 2000; Hodkinson *et al.*, 1996).

Cultural explanations have been resisted strongly by those who emphasize the role of intellectual ability (allied with hard work) as a pure and independent variable, a genetic inheritance that transcends nurture, culture and society. They claim that intelligence (IQ[14]) is 80 per cent heritable, that compensatory education has failed, and that genetic factors are of overwhelming importance in producing intellectual differences (Jensen, 1969; Eysenck, 1971). *The Bell Curve* (Herrnstein and Murray, 1994) argued that IQ is a more important determinant of a person's success in adulthood than the socio-economic status of his or her parents, but the book provoked a hostile reaction by discussing the implications of racial differences in intelligence. Saunders (2010) believes that ability and motivation matter more than class in predicting someone's occupational future and that although some people still enjoy relative advantage, we are nearer to a meritocratic society than many imagine. Intelligence or 'brightness' is often presented as if it were a stable and independent characteristic, unaffected by life circumstances and experience but open to rapid growth provided an appropriately high-quality education is provided (Henry, 2013).

Arguments such as these have become increasingly difficult to sustain. IQ tests are supposed to provide a pure and timeless measure of intelligence, but they have been subject to their own version of grade inflation. Massive IQ gains have been found in twenty industrialized countries, equivalent to an average 15 points or one standard deviation per generation. These gains are too big to be equated with real improvements in ability and show that intelligence is harder to theorize than previously thought (Roemer, 2000). Heritability has been over-estimated in studies restricted to twins (Feldman *et al.*, 2000), measured intelligence has been found to explain no more than 15 to 30 per cent of the variation in US students' high school grades (DiMaggio, 1982), and the vast majority of reported variations in attained class and class mobility are not accounted for by IQ. Many other factors, including personality characteristics, values and health, as well as contingent events, have a strong role (Nettle, 2003). A later review of the evidence presented in *The Bell Curve* suggests that, contrary to Herrnstein and Murray's assertions, parental family background may be more important than IQ in shaping social and economic success in adulthood (Sanders, Korenman and Winship, 2000).

Recent studies have further emphasized the role of family background and early experience in accounting for differences in children's responses to school and subsequent opportunities. NEP (2010) found, for example, that an extra £100 per month in income when children were young was associated with a difference equivalent to one month's development. This dissimilarity was not fixed at birth but widened through childhood. Data from the MCS has been analysed to reveal that differences in children's intellectual, emotional and behavioural development, by parental income group, emerge at an early stage, as soon as the third birthday, and have great significance for their later achievements. The family is believed to be the principal social institution that fosters income inequality (Ermisch and Francesconi, 2002; Ermisch, 2008).

There is a growing sense that 'natural' ability cannot be separated empirically from 'cultural capital' (Scherger and Savage, 2010). Ability and talent seem to be not the innate, fixed attributes of a limited number of people, but genetic potentials that must be activated and nurtured through experience. Children form trillions of synapses as they adapt to their environment but, from the age of 8, unused neurons are discarded and lost. 'Concerted cultivation' provides the opportunity, stimulus and practice without which native potential may be undeveloped or wasted, while small family advantages increase the chance of long-term success. This adaptive conception of ability confirms the importance of social and cultural influences on human growth and development (Smail, 2008; Barker, 2011).

Inequality

Until recently, disadvantage was believed to stem from material deprivation. Hardship seemed to reduce the social capital available to many families in poor urban districts and to limit children's ability to perform well at school (Machin, 1999). New Labour responded with numerous area-based initiatives (e.g. Sure Start, Excellence in Cities, Full Service Extended Schools) that provided compensatory resources and services to support, re-educate and re-socialize working-class families left behind by the general rise in prosperity (Raffo, 2011). Poor people were pathologized as an 'unknowing uncritical tasteless mass' that needed support to compete effectively at school and in the labour market (Gewirtz, 2001; Reay, 2006: 295). The difficulty with this understanding is that poverty and deprivation are widely if unevenly distributed throughout the UK, and seem to be an endemic feature of the British economy, rather than dysfunctional occurrences confined to inner city environments (Barker, 2011).

We are now recovering the idea that disadvantage and deprivation are relative terms, and that relational variables (e.g. the degree of inequality in a particular society) are much more important for human health and happiness than the material conditions in which people live, unless these fail to meet basic needs. We are beginning to understand that our relative status, and the relative steepness of the social gradient to which we belong, are profoundly important for our individual and collective welfare. Wilkinson and Pickett's (2009) epidemiological study of inequality has three main elements. In the first, they compare the income spread in 21 advanced countries, using the Gini coefficient,[15] with each country's index rating on ten health and social problems. Figure 2.2 shows the results, with the least unequal countries experiencing significantly better outcomes than the more unequal countries.

The second element repeats this analysis with comparable data from the states that comprise the US. This study confirms the relationship between high inequality and greater health and social problems, with the least unequal states having better outcomes than more unequal states. Wilkinson and Pickett conclude that the gradient of income inequality in a state can be used to estimate accurately the incidence of health and other problems in that state. They show that 'international educational scores are closely related to income inequality' and that 'more unequal states have worse educational attainment' (2010: 105).

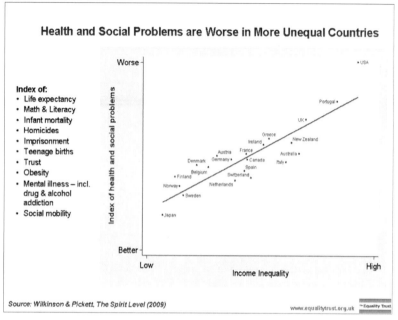

Figure 2.2: Income inequality compared with health and social problems
(Wilkinson and Pickett, 2009)

The final element draws together a large number of health studies that confirm the negative impact of social inequality. Increased inequality produces heightened anxiety, evaluative threats to the social self, reduced self-esteem, greater social insecurity and more status-related shame. Innumerable studies reveal that each of these has a marked impact on health, including life expectancy. The incidence of problems does not relate to average income levels or particular levels of disadvantage but to the spread of income across the social gradient. Everyone is better off in more equal societies. This is a troubling finding for the UK, where income inequality has increased dramatically since 1974 and is among the highest in the world.

Wilkinson and Pickett (2009) argue that inequality and the resulting disadvantage are not shaped by levels of material deprivation, or confined to a particular location or community, but are instead features of human society that condition everyone's health and happiness. For them, education is just another area where inequality exerts a formative influence, not an agent that improves life chances or overcomes social problems. Schools may help a few fortunate individuals achieve upward mobility, but they cannot overcome disadvantage as a phenomenon, however efficient and effective they may become (Equality Trust, 2012; Wilkinson and Pickett, 2009). As Crawford *et al.* (2011) conclude in a review for the Department for Business, Innovation and Skills, it is very hard to increase social mobility without tackling inequality.

Social reproduction?

Despite these alternative perspectives, policy-makers continue to believe that family, class, culture and inequality are barriers to overcome, rather than intermingling influences that shape young people's growth and development. From this individualist standpoint, hardworking students can achieve good qualifications and rise to the highest positions society has to offer, provided they have access to an education that 'matches the best in the independent sector' (HMG 2011: 38). The new academies, set up to be as independent as schools and colleges in the private sector, are expected to emulate the curriculum offered by elite institutions, raise standards and so minimize the gaps between students from different backgrounds. This is how Gove plans to counter 'the sheer scale, the breadth and the depth of private school dominance of our society' and so improve social mobility (Gove, 2012, unpaged).

As we have seen, however, there is historical evidence that the school system tends towards social reproduction rather than transformation, with status, wealth and education woven together in persistent and even predictable patterns of advantage and disadvantage. Despite thoroughgoing reorganization in the 1960s and 1970s, and the proliferation of school formats in the 1990s and 2000s,[16] the system is today as 'stratified and segregated' as ever, with graduated variations in income, resources and selectivity at every level (DfE, 2010b: 1). The disparity between schools in terms of their wealth, facilities and per-student income is immense. The boarding fees at Sevenoaks School, for example, are advertised at £29,610 per pupil, per year. The day fees, at £18,459 per head, are 37 per cent greater than the average cost for independent schooling, and 300 per cent higher than mean state expenditure per pupil (Chowdry and Sibieta, 2011; Sevenoaks School, 2012).

One head has recently warned that private schools risk becoming the 'sole preserve of the super-rich', while Martin Stephen, ex-High Master of St Paul's School, says the very top schools are becoming as 'socially exclusive' as they were in the Victorian era because of rising fee levels. Substantial social, economic and cultural capital is required to gain admission to the leading independent schools, with selection achieved through a subtle blend of competitive examinations, parental wealth and prior schooling[17] (Paton, 2012, unpaged). Despite many shared advantages, however, there are marked performance variations within the private sector. *The Guardian* league table ranks 475 independent schools by GCSE points score per candidate, which range from 81.3 at St Paul's School to 26.3 at Stanbridge Earls School (*Guardian*, 2011). Is it reasonable to expect non-selective, low-budget comprehensives to match elite results when most independents themselves struggle to compete with the leading schools in their sector? How can an inner-city academy that remains poor and comprehensive hope to emulate the experience and outcomes offered by the best fee-paying schools? Can more rigorous curriculum and assessment arrangements make that much difference?

The leading independent schools may be more exclusive than others but the process of social differentiation has been observed at work in every context. An evaluation of the assisted places scheme in the 1980s found that most members of the better-placed middle class chose elite schools, while those in lower socio-economic groups, though still counted as members of the middle class, tended towards the lower end of the hierarchy. First choice of university was also class-based, with students from managerial and intermediate backgrounds more likely to select a local higher education institution where they would be close to friends and family. When less-elite members of the middle class did achieve top grades, they felt that Oxbridge was not for them (Power *et al.*, 2003).

Those who attended private schools were more likely to study traditional academic subjects and to attend elite institutions. Although 93 per cent of the evaluation's informants were in non-manual jobs, with 75 per cent in professional or managerial occupations, the authors reported a close association of parental education and status with the educational achievements and occupational destination of their children. Their conclusion is that 'England has moved towards a "class meritocracy" – a divided system that is both meritocratic and socially exclusive' (Power *et al.*, 2003: 151).

Ball (2003a) has found similar evidence of social stratification and differentiation, and documents the ways in which middle-class families have exploited the open enrolment system created by the 1988 Education Act. Parents have engaged in the 'micropractices of social reproduction and the situated enactment of class skills, resources, dispositions, attitudes and expectations' to secure relative advantage for their children (Ball, 2003a: 3). The cumulative effect of these manoeuvres has been to create or confirm local hierarchies of schooling rather than to close the results gap between effective and less effective institutions. Schools in the lower regions of the local school hierarchy have higher concentrations of socially disadvantaged students relative to their neighbours, and so find it difficult to improve their results. Those in the upper reaches of the hierarchy are more successful at public examinations, mainly because they draw their students from more prosperous families (Levačić and Woods, 2002).

The problem seems to be that children from poor backgrounds tend to achieve less than their peers, regardless of the school attended, and that schools with significant numbers of disadvantaged children are likely to perform less well than those with fewer poor children. The persistent attainment gap between rich and poor students is similar for most schools, so the social mobility problem is not that weak schools are failing disadvantaged students, but that poor children do much less well almost everywhere. This picture emerges from *Financial Times* data presented in figure 2.3. The upper, heavy line shows the average point score for students in each percentile of schools, with results improving from left to right. The lower, light line shows the average point score, but only for poorer children within those schools.[18] The upper line climbs rapidly as average performance improves, but the lower line remains flat and does not cross the national average line until the 85th percentile. The conclusion is that high-performing schools are no more likely to close the gap than low performers, and that poverty remains strikingly resistant to school-level interventions (Cook, 2012).

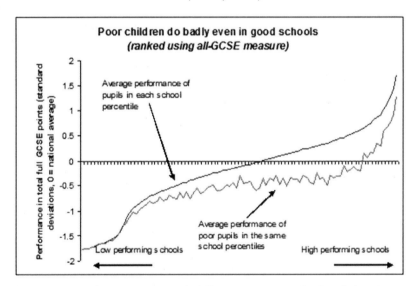

Figure 2.3: Performance in total full GCSE points, displayed by average performance of all pupils in each school percentile, compared with average performance of poor pupils in the same school percentiles (Cook, 2012)

The main reason for the success of our 'best' schools seems to be that status and selection make them quite literally exclusive, so that relatively poor children are diverted to suitable establishments nearer to home. This may be why the introduction and expansion of universal education systems in the UK and Western Europe has not led to increasing levels of social mobility. Educational attainment may be linked closely to income levels and the social class that individuals achieve, but educational achievement is itself linked strongly to social class origins (Nunn *et al.*, 2007).

Closing gaps

A broad trend towards social reproduction does not mean that individuals from less-advantaged backgrounds are unable to achieve good academic results and progress towards high-status jobs. Those with service-class backgrounds may have a much better chance of achieving a service-class job than those from manual backgrounds, for example, but an accumulation of small advantages can equip individuals to exceed even their own expectations. The considerable social fluidity observed in western economies provides ample scope for individualism to work for individuals (Heath and Payne, 2000; Savage, 2000; Dasgupta, 2010).

The Coalition has more ambitious plans, however. Michael Gove is passionate about creating a general improvement in academic standards and future mobility that will transcend family background. The difficulty is that the small advantages that favour some individuals and families are hard to generalize across the whole population. The formation of family capital is beyond bureaucratic control and is not easily increased by external intervention. In addition, the education system has intrinsic features that work against the government's overall aim of raising standards and closing or reducing the attainment gap between students from different backgrounds.

School standards are measured by the proportion of students matching a prescribed grade threshold across a range of subjects (e.g. 5 GCSEs at grades A*–C), and policy-makers speak as though results on current tests and examinations belong to an objective framework that enables attainment to be monitored and improved over time. This involves ignoring a wide range of statistical and technical problems as well as the instability of the assessment methods used (Goldstein, 2001). Gove's recent alterations to the criteria used to judge school performance follow many other changes since the introduction of GCSEs in 1987 and expose the subjective nature of decisions about what is to be valued and rewarded.

Frequent changes in curriculum, mode of assessment, grade boundaries and performance criteria mean there is no realistic prospect of a valid comparison between annual sets of examination results (Goldstein, 2001; Goldstein and Thomas, 1996). Although Gove claims his curriculum and assessment reforms have greater validity than those preceding them, the radical plans he advocates seem no more than a salvo in a continuous struggle over educational aims and objectives. There is no agreed standard by which improvements in the quality and relevance of education may be judged, only tests and examinations that reflect the values and priorities of government agencies (Ball, 2003b; Mansell, 2007, 2011; Barker, 2010a, 2013).

Attainment does not relate to a defined standard, therefore, but to the marks students obtain on test and examination papers. Candidates are ranked according to their total marks, producing a pattern that resembles a bell or normal distribution curve. Many biological, psychological and social phenomena occur in a population in this distribution, so the continuous black curve on figure 2.4 represents an expectation of the results pattern to be expected in any test or examination. Examiners decide where grade boundaries should be drawn and grades are awarded according to a candidate's position on the distribution curve. Provided grade boundaries remain the same, there is no room for teachers to improve grades and overall performance or for politicians to claim that standards have risen or fallen.

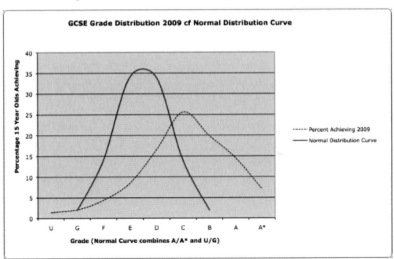

Figure 2.4: GCSE grade distribution in 2009 compared with the normal distribution curve (Barker, 2010b: 156)

Grade boundaries have proved flexible, however, and over time have departed from the expected normal distribution. The grade distribution for 2009 (see the dotted line on the figure) indicates that, for reasons unknown, marks are now converted into grades more generously than they were in the past. The proportion achieving A or A* GCSE grades has risen, for example, from 8.4 per cent in 1988 to 22.4 per cent in 2012 (Datablog, 2012). This apparent improvement provides reliable information about shifting grade boundaries but tells us nothing about whether students that year achieved higher standards, whether the questions were easier, or whether the whole process has been corrupted by hyper-accountability and the drive to produce ever better results (Mansell, 2007). Gove's new, improved qualifications are supposed to resolve these questions, but he has not explained how 'standards' can be tracked and raised by using data from norm-referenced examination papers. Like his predecessors he has set targets (floor standards) that can be achieved only through the manipulation of boundaries to increase the volume of higher grades awarded. The education secretary's desire to prevent grade inflation, and to increase the value of his revised GCSE qualification, may initially reduce the proportion attaining good grades, but in the longer run the political imperative to improve results will be unchanged. The new regime, however rigorous, seems set to employ the same flawed techniques as the old (Mansell, 2011).

Social inclusion and social mobility are thwarted, therefore, by an assessment system that emphasizes relative examination performance. Students are filtered and sorted by reference to the normal distribution curve, regardless of how hard they work and how able they may be. The statistical methods employed rank students rather than assessing their progress. The use of grades converts the bell curve into an eight-point hierarchy (A to U) that exaggerates small variations around the mean and reproduces the harsh gradient of the social order. This helps explain why schools have such difficulty in reducing the relative performance differences between social groups. Gove hopes this will change when every school is as good as the best in the private sector, but if everyone receives an equally effective education, the stratification of achievement by social class may become even greater than it is now. Those with the most social and cultural capital may do even better, so widening the gap rather than closing it (Mortimore and Whitty, 2000).

These systemic flaws have been masked since 1988 by increased participation and by the shift of grade boundaries towards better and better results. But the growth in educational credentials has achieved less than expected. There is little sign that productivity and skills have increased because of the growth in qualifications, and the inflation of credentials seems to have produced competition between status groups rather than greater efficiency and output (Brown, 2001; Collins, 1981). When the general increase in qualifications is taken into account, there has been little change in the effects of attainment on occupational status. Despite improved opportunities to gain qualifications, there remains a strong association between class origin and class destination (Jackson, 2007; 2009).

Understanding mobility – habitus, field and institutional habitus

In our hearts we are individualists, to a greater or lesser degree confident in our power to shape the course of our lives and to make a difference in the lives of others. But the eclectic ideas and concepts discussed above – relative advantage, social class, cultural capital, inequality and social reproduction – help us recognize the myriad influences that bear on our personal growth and on our interactions with other human beings. These perspectives suggest the variety and complexity of the whispering networks that condition people's life trajectories, but their diversity limits their theoretical usefulness.

They do not resolve enduring questions about the relationship between education and social mobility and leave us unsure about the extent to which students from lower-class backgrounds achieve the meritocratic dream, with or without the Pupil Premium. The possibility remains that increased mobility may have an unintended but negative impact, with inequality sharpening as talented individuals are removed from struggling communities. There is the further risk that we are rushing to improve mobility without understanding it. A study in the 1970s found that many working-class people have a negative evaluation of middle-class careers and lifestyles and have little enthusiasm for moving up. Most respondents were well integrated into their class and community and were, to a degree, blinkered in conforming to family expectations. Short-distance mobility, to adjacent occupational categories, was far more common than extreme movement between classes. But those who were upwardly mobile seem to have been at odds with their environment from early childhood and had proved themselves unusual in being ready to take risks in challenging and unpredictable conditions. Oddly, they showed no interest in striving for status (Richardson, 1977).

This encounter with incomplete theory and insecure knowledge has prompted us to concentrate our attention on the interplay of agency and structure in our respondents' personal stories and trajectories, and to interpret their perceptions in the light of Bourdieu's (1977a) concepts of habitus, field and institutional habitus (see chapter 1). We believe the concept of habitus provides ways to explore the tension between individual agency and wider societal structures, despite criticisms that habitus is latently deterministic (Calhoun *et al.*, 1993). We agree with Reay (2004: 439) that 'first and foremost habitus is a conceptual tool to be used in empirical research rather than an idea to be debated in texts', and assess the extent to which our respondents have the capacity to choose and act within the social and material settings in which they operate (Mills, 2008).

Notes

[1] Margaret Thatcher, UK Prime Minister, 1979–1990.

[2] The Pupil Premium aims to provide an extra £2.5 billion per year for pupils who receive FSM (HMG, 2011: 6).

[3] The *service class* refers to classes I and II in Goldthorpe's (1987) social classification and includes professional, managerial and high-level administrative positions, as well as the owners of large companies.

[4] Absolute mobility rates measure the proportion of individuals ending up in a higher social class than their parents. Increased absolute mobility may show a lot of movement, but does not show distinctions between movement caused by changes in the occupational system itself and movement resulting from greater fluidity between occupational groups.

[5] Relative mobility rates indicate an individual's chances of movement into a higher social class.

[6] This is Gove's term (2012, unpaged).

[7] Kulaks were farmers impoverished by the communist authorities during their persecution of the landed peasantry in the early 1950s.

[8] The top 10 per cent of households have 97 times as much wealth as the bottom 10 per cent (NEP, 2010).

[9] Targets are now expressed as 'floor standards'.

[10] The chart was constructed by giving every 16-year-old who took GCSEs at a state school in 2010 a point score for their examination performance, with 8 points for an A* down to 1 point for a G. The data was standardized and displayed by the relative wealth of their neighbourhoods, with children living in deprived postcodes at the left of the chart and those in the richest on the right.

[11] The Assisted Places scheme was introduced in 1980. Some students whose parents could not afford independent education were provided with free or subsidised places.

[12] The survey was based on a theory developed by Pierre Bourdieu in 1984. It looked at a person's cultural and social life as well as economic status. Participants indicated whether they enjoyed any of 27 cultural activities, including watching opera and going to the gym.

[13] This study draws on large-scale data sets, including the Millennium Cohort Study (MCS), the Avon Longitudinal Study of Parents and Children (ALSPAC), the Longitudinal Study of Young People in England (LSYPE) and the British Cohort Study (BCS). The children involved were observed from early childhood through to late adolescence.

[14] The Gini coefficient is a widely-used measure of inequality across a whole society (Wilkinson and Pickett, 2009: 17–18).

[15] A person's intelligence quotient or IQ is conceived as a measure of relative ability.

[16] This included specialist schools, faith schools, trust schools and academies.

[17] Socially and academically selective preparatory schools provide a high proportion of pupils at the leading boarding schools, for example.

[18] The poor children included in the chart are those living in the lowest fifth of households, as measured by the deprivation of the postcode.

Chapter 3
Schools and achievement

Introduction

As chapter 2 discussed, in recent decades governments of centre-left and centre-right, influenced by broad trends in the global economy, have come to view education as a primary source of added value and competitive advantage. Chapter 3 begins by considering the quality of provision in two high-performing schools. The students overwhelmingly refer to the schools and teachers in positive ways and describe their delight in teachers who engage their attention and interest. However, despite years of government initiatives that are supposed to achieve classroom consistency, there is also some evidence of less-satisfactory teaching, even in these good or outstanding schools.

Since the early 1980s successive governments have emphasized the important role that education plays in improving social mobility. They have stressed its potential to sweep away obstacles to future mobility, and thus to facilitate future fairness and economic efficiency for the country (DfE, 2010a). To illustrate some of the issues associated with taking this rational and objective view of social mobility, chapter 3 explores the extent to which the students at South Park and Felix Holt are ambitious for themselves, in terms of the competitive individualist model. Drawing on habitus and field, the chapter also considers how much the respondents desire and seek educational and career goals associated with becoming mobile or reproducing their class position. These discussions highlight the respondents' investment in an individualist model of success and demonstrate respondents' beliefs that being competitive will help them to achieve the right grades to take their desired next steps.

The chapter then considers the ways in which these students believe they are 'authors of their own lives' who work hard to reach challenging goals and targets. They tend to have optimistic plans for their future employment. The only external constraint they acknowledged was the possibility of not obtaining the right grades to pursue a preferred education and employment pathway. The chapter highlights their beliefs that social class, ethnicity and gender are not significant barriers to future progress. The respondents dismissed the possibility that their identities could affect their future pathways.

Quality of provision

There is abundant evidence that teaching is excellent at both schools and that it enables students to outperform local and national expectations. Ofsted reports and relative examination success show continuous improvement over time, and confirm that students have access to high-quality education across the ability spectrum. At Felix Holt, in 2011, Ofsted rated outcomes for individuals and for groups of pupils as outstanding (grade 1) and reported that: 'students' achievement is good … there is no significant difference in the progress of different groups of students. Very high specialist targets are now close to being met. Expectations are high and students enjoy a challenge.' Post-16 results were also good, with 70 per cent of year 13 students achieving three A level passes in 2011 (Felix Holt Ofsted report 2011; BBC, 2012a). An assistant head with sixth form responsibility emphasized the school's determination to raise aspirations:

> We show comprehensive school kids can aspire to and attain entry to top universities, including Oxbridge. There's been a year-on-year rise in the numbers going to university; 79 students from a year 13 of approximately 130 gained admission in 2012. Already there are 86 applications, not including the kids who apply for foundation art courses. This year and the year before 30 to 35 individuals have secured Russell Group offers; when I came into my sixth form role I pushed Russell Group massively.

South Park's 2011 results were likewise very good, with 67 per cent of students achieving 5 or more A*–C GCSE grades, including English and mathematics. This represents an 11 per cent advance since 2007, greater than the 8 per cent increase in the proportion of students attaining this criterion nationally over the last four years. In 2012, Ofsted's interim assessment found that, since the 2008 full inspection, the school's good (grade 2) performance 'has been sustained and that we can defer its next full inspection' (South Park Ofsted interim assessment, 2012: 2).

Students in A and B groups were equally positive about their education, in ways that confirmed external judgements about the quality of provision. South Park A group respondents described their school in glowing terms. Clare said the school is very good compared with local state schools and even with nearby private schools. Adam said he would be hard pressed to find a better school. Jacob praised the music and drama departments in particular and was doubtful that he would have had the same kind of teaching from other schools. Emma emphasized the supportive culture she experienced:

'If you don't understand, you can get people to help or talk you through – teachers and pupils are there to help you and take time and trouble'.

South Park B group respondents were also pleased with the school. Isaac claimed the school was 'one of the best in England'. Jordan emphasized South Park's good reputation 'around the county' and Jasmine remarked that there were 'a lot of friendly teachers, with whom revising and learning is fun'. Samantha felt that the school was helpful and encouraging.

Felix Holt students were equally satisfied with their school. Adele contrasted her previous school with Felix Holt, where she said people were more accepting of individuals and did not try to fit newcomers into a mould. Instead, the atmosphere was very encouraging. She said the school's local reputation is deservedly high: 'The community admires the school, all the parents want their kids to come here, students are encouraged to get involved in the community and volunteer, so the school is perceived to do its bit'.

Martin was very enthusiastic and spoke for many when he said: 'This school is amazing'. Paul agreed that Felix Holt was 'absolutely fantastic' and believed that its 'terrific reputation' is well justified.

Less academically successful group B students were no less inclined to praise their school. Although Darren was repeating year 13, he was as enthusiastic as anyone about his educational experience: 'School has been brilliant for me; the quality of teaching is very good'. Harry was repeating year 12 but nevertheless thought the school was very good. He said the standard of teaching had improved a lot since he started: 'They give you a lot of support from an early stage to achieve your goals, especially in the sixth form where the teachers become a friend to you for what you need'. These high-performing schools emphasize excellent teaching, high expectations and achievement for their students, and the fact that they fulfil these aims is evidenced in their Ofsted reports.

The influence of teachers

Many respondents heaped praise on the teachers who were pushing, supporting and nurturing their academic talents. The students described their delight in teachers who engaged their attention and interest. But a number of respondents also reported that they had experienced what they described as less-satisfactory teaching, even in these outstanding schools. Students described their difficulties with less-capable and less-aware members of staff. They were highly critical of teachers they identified as failing to hold their focus and attention, or to provide them with challenging lessons and goals to enable them to achieve their examination potential.

Positive

Students at Felix Holt and South Park were generally comfortable with their teachers, confident about the relevance and usefulness of their education, and endorsed their schools' targets and goals without reservation. Respondents were optimistic, and positive about themselves and about their prospects in education, even when they expected to receive below-average grades. Although many of those interviewed referred to financial hardship, family problems (such as separation, divorce and ill health) and relative disadvantage, they perceived difficulties as challenges to overcome, not obstacles to complain about. Even the less able, less fortunate students who were expected to achieve modest results believed that examinations were important for career success, and emphasized their own agency in achieving personal goals.

Teachers were generally depicted as enablers who provided opportunities for the students. Many were seen as key sponsors, putting students forward for clubs and groups and helping them to realize their potential. In the Felix Holt A group, Rebecca commented that her teachers often provided students with opportunities to develop their academic and employability skills. Gemma said the 'teachers have given me so many opportunities, they helped with my university application and they sent me to summer school and even fixed work experience for me at Glaxo'. She felt that, because some of her teachers had studied at Oxford and Cambridge, they had been able to help and support her high academic aspirations. Tom told us that most teachers were supportive, and Ben said many were brilliant in a range of areas of the curriculum. Kylie credited her teachers with 'helping me to acquire skills to get into college' and Paul said that teachers were 'fantastic, personable and supportive, they'll help even when it's not their field'. Jack said that teachers gave him lots of time and support.

Felix Holt B group students also praised and admired their teachers. Craig commented that 'you have bonds with teachers who have a huge impact on your life and where you are heading and it makes it easier for you as a student to follow'. Holly said that, in her experience, the teachers 'try their best to help you do what you want to do and they try to fit in extra help with courses'. Marilyn thought the teaching standards were high, and Tania and Claudia concurred with this view. Daniel told us that teaching staff were interested in helping the students and wanted the best for them. Dean, Simon, Matt and Craig reported strong bonds with teachers who had supported their academic development. Lauren cited the positive influence of teachers as a determining factor in her decision to stay at Felix Holt:

I was going to leave for a different sixth form, I decided not to because of my friendships with many of the teachers, I felt I'd have their support and wouldn't have to work so hard to make friends or earn teachers' trust.

Harry thought the standard of teaching had improved considerably since he had joined the school, and Darren had experienced excellent teaching since he had joined the sixth form.

The warm comments made about the teachers by the students in the South Park A group were often peppered with more negative views (discussed below). But three students were overwhelmingly positive. Adam said that, in his experience, the teachers were lovely. Clare agreed and told us 'the teachers are good at teaching, they are good at their subjects and they try to motivate us'. Jason identified several outstanding teachers who had supported and helped him.

Gary, Kathy and Jasmine (South Park B group) said the teachers were generally good and supportive. Anna felt that overall the teaching was good. Isaac had experienced teachers who would 'give up time to help'. Jordan also noted that 'there are always teachers there if you need help and they are available at lunchtime'. Max thought highly of the teachers, some of whom had 'helped me through thick and thin'. Leah could not praise the teachers enough and told us 'the teachers are absolutely amazing, every year the students improve, so teachers are learning what to do better'. Alison particularly valued extra-curricular clubs and competitions as well as extra tuition at lunchtime; she identified these as important for developing and extending her opportunities to secure future employment. Patrick offered his view:

> This is a very positive school. If you are under-achieving they'll provide extra support, with extra revision at lunchtime. I do geography and English at lunchtime and after school, and it's really helping. There are a lot less of us at lunchtime, with only five in the geography revision group, for example, so you get a lot of one-to-one help with stuff you don't understand.

Patrick is a good example of a student who benefitted from receiving extra support with revision to ensure he could secure the examination grades needed to pursue his preferred higher education pathway. The teachers, senior leaders and head teacher were all committed to academic excellence and worked hard to ensure that students had a range of opportunities to pursue activities that complemented their formal academic learning, such as revision groups in all subject areas.

A and B group members in both schools told us that receiving positive input, belief, support and engaging pedagogic experiences from a teacher were important factors in their subject choices and examination success. For example, Gemma attributed her decision to continue with dance and drama into her GCSE years to her teachers: 'If you really like your teachers it will make you more keen on the subject and the way they teach it'. Michael said that teachers were the 'biggest influence on my art'. Julian said he has improved 'because the teachers have pushed me and kept me working hard, they knew I had the potential'. Alison appreciated the availability of her teachers: 'There are always teachers there if you need help. You've got tutors to help if there are any problems.'

Teachers were important in pushing the students on to achieve their potential. They emphasized the importance of hard work and focus in their pupils' efforts to secure future academic and employment success. They often worked with parents to reinforce messages about hard work and competition as important ways of securing access to educational and economic goods, with little mention of the hindrance that structural inequalities could present. This outlook seems optimistic in the context of well-rehearsed arguments about the shrinking middle-class economy and changing forms of employment (Allen and Ainley, 2010).

Critical

But several students in both schools were critical of the quality of teaching and learning and of their teachers' behaviour management, and expressed frustration at being patronized by teachers. In the South Park A group, Rose found it 'weird' that there were 'loads of outstanding teachers and lots of poor teachers' and Faith and Jason were unhappy with teachers who struggled to control a class. Hannah, Noah and Zoey agreed with Clare's estimate that 'about two-thirds are really good and there's a minority that aren't so great'. Ellie thought that less good teachers were perceived as bad because students' expectations were so high, especially in the top sets. Isabella said she had good teachers who were making a real difference compared with the previous year, especially in mathematics. Chloe and Sean reported a mixed picture, with areas of good teaching and others that were less good, and both students identified several good and several bad teachers.

In the South Park B group there was evidence of some frustration at the influence of a few teachers. Jasmine talked about her negative experience with teachers who 'tell you you [sic] are going to fail and apply pressure, it makes you worry about your grades'. Sharon talked about her frustration with one 'good teacher ... but he has no control of a group of boys', and Anna thought that the school was good but with a few low points in terms of the quality of some of her teachers.

Ben was the only student in the Felix Holt A group who was generally critical of his teaching. He explained his view on the teachers as follows:

> I've had less good experiences too ... you can be treated more childishly, with less responsibility, and that I didn't like. One of my [...] teachers previously paid little attention to the class, he was quite lazy ... He gets annoyed because we're lazy when we were just reflecting what he was doing.

In the Felix Holt B group Emilio told us that the quality of teaching varied throughout the subjects and 'one or two teachers are a bit boring and stick a PowerPoint up and make you copy down notes'. Tony and Dave felt a little patronized by the teachers who did not treat them as adults. They expressed frustration towards some of the school's rules, such as the requirement to sign in at 9am on Tuesdays even though there was no lesson until 11am. Both students had part-time evening jobs to support their full-time education and would have liked more sleep.

These critical remarks, offered in the main by high-achieving students in the context of general respect for the quality of education at South Park, suggest that Michael Gove is right to emphasize the importance of teaching. Students have been encouraged to aim high and work hard, but without the support of 'really good teachers' their efforts are unlikely to produce the desired results. Teachers must play a crucial role in any plan to improve social mobility because they encourage young people to be ambitious and provide practical help with progression.

Disengaged

Despite being located in outstanding schools with comfortable material conditions and generally prosperous, if diverse, local neighbourhoods, two students rejected an academic curriculum that seemed irrelevant to their lives and distanced themselves from their teachers and classmates. Sandy (South Park B group) offered strenuous criticism of her school and teachers, and of their impact on her life:

> The school is holding me back. It seems only to take notice of the pupils who have high grades, they expect people of our standard to be the ones who are not successful or have a less good life but

I think we have a better life than those who spend all their time revising and studying when they could do it anyway.

Sandy was frustrated by the teachers' focus on the academic students in her cohort and reflected a sense of marginalization within the formal education system, in which she perceived that she did not receive sufficient support and encouragement for her vocational aspirations. It was evident throughout the interview that Sandy had little empathy with her classmates and teachers, and presented herself as leading an enjoyable, independent, almost adult life. She worked part time in her mother's hair salon, went out with boyfriends, and enjoyed 'getting smashed' most weekends. She saw no value in the school curriculum as she experienced it: 'It's got repetitive. What use is French I'll never use? I'm not into language, I don't care about the subject, I'll never understand it. It's a waste of my time.' Her story illustrated the limitations of the contemporary education context where the focus is on academic education at the expense of more vocational and practical pathways. These pathways are undergoing significant changes following the Wolf Report (Department for Education and Department for Business, Innovation & Skills, 2011), which sets out the benefits of some of the current vocational training available but also criticizes significant elements of existing provision. Gavin shared this perspective and was the only male participant to express dissatisfaction. He commented that he was fed up because he felt he had learned enough, and wanted to get on with his life. Revision, he said, was boring and the constant repetition felt like a waste of time.

Gavin and Sandy's sense of alienation from the curriculum and their teachers raises questions about the possibilities for those students who come from disadvantaged backgrounds, especially those with generally low academic aspirations. What sorts of pathway are available to students from these families? The psychological, emotional and material steps required to follow an academic or high-status vocational pathway are well documented (Mahony and Zmroczek, 1997; Ball *et al.*, 2000; Archer *et al.*, 2010). These studies illustrate the difficulty facing those students who do not possess academic aspirations, middle-class dispositions or valued forms of social and cultural capital.

Sandy's strong opinions and personal agenda, based on helping with her mother's business, earning money and having fun, were at variance with every other student at South Park except Gavin. Nobody at Felix Holt articulated a comparable resentment or reflected on class differences between themselves and their teachers. Sandy and Gavin were the only individuals in our study to resemble the disadvantaged participants in Reay's account of *The Zombie Stalking English Schools*:

> Kenny: Some teachers are a bit snobby, sort of. And some teachers act as if the child is stupid. Because they've got a posh accent. Like they talk without 'innits' and 'mans', like they talk proper English. And they say, 'That isn't the way you talk' – like putting you down. Like I think telling you a different way is sort of good, but I think the way they do it isn't good because they correct you and make you look stupid.
>
> Martin: Those teachers look down on you.
>
> Kenny: Yeah, like they think you're dumb ... we don't expect them to treat us like their own children. We're not. But we are still kids. I'd say to them, 'You've got kids. You treat them with love but you don't need to love us. All you need to do is treat us like humans.'
>
> (Reay, 2006: 297)

Our data contains little sense of the 'hidden injuries of class' believed to be enshrined and perpetuated by educational policy (Sennett and Cobb, 1972). There is no hint of the damage supposedly generated by the increased surveillance and regulation of pupils' learning, although many respondents in each school described straitened family budgets and disadvantaged personal circumstances (Beckmann and Cooper, 2005).

The contrast between student attitudes at our two schools and those reported at locations with high concentrations of disadvantage may be accounted for in several ways. Intake mix is believed to have a marked influence on school processes, so social composition may help explain the scarcity of negative attitudes at Felix Holt and South Park (Thrupp, 1999; Levačić and Woods, 2002). FSM uptake at both schools is well below the national average and each has a long history as a full-range comprehensive with a balanced intake drawn from mixed urban, suburban and rural environments. Students from less-advantaged social backgrounds may benefit from belonging to more mixed communities that enjoy a lower population density.

Policy-makers, however, are inclined to dismiss the role of disadvantage altogether, and argue powerfully that schools have a formative impact on behaviour and outcomes. They interpret the positive attitudes and outlook found at schools like Felix Holt and South Park as signs of progress towards equal opportunities, improved education and increased social mobility (Adonis, 2012; Barber, 2008). Be that as it may, our respondents are convinced that their schools are effective, and that nothing in their personal circumstances need hold them back, provided they work hard and achieve good qualifications relevant to their aspirations (see chapter 5). From the government's perspective, this is welcome evidence that good schools can provide fair access to education, so improving life chances and encouraging social mobility.

An important motivation for the respondents' desire to achieve their potential in the education market related to their plans for securing an economically prosperous future through hard work and application.

Hard work

The students' discussions about their plans for their future careers suggest that they believe them to be entirely in their own hands and achievable through hard work. The only external constraint they acknowledged was the possibility that they would not obtain the right grades to pursue a preferred education or employment pathway. Social class, ethnicity and gender were not perceived to be significant barriers to future progress and, in the interviews, they denied that these had any impact. Their responses to questions about the possible impact of identity on their pathways very much reflected the attitude that there was 'no problem here' (see Gaine, 1995).

They reported their belief that, with hard work, dedication and application, they would be able to gain the examination grades to enable them to take up places at a desired university, vocational course or apprenticeship scheme. In this way, they reflected government ideals and discourses, articulated over the past 25 years, that have emphasized that success and failure rely on the commitment and determination of the individual (Barker, 2012; Hoskins, 2012a). This entrenched position reflects the view of schooling as a meritocracy where rewards are meted out in accordance with effort. As the discussion in this section illustrates, there is no acknowledgement of the impact that structural inequalities can have on the individual. Certain ethnic or class positions can affect individual outcomes and gender inequality presents particular challenges to young women seeking a professional career and family life in the future (Hoskins, 2012b); nonetheless, the respondents in our study without exception believe that they can steer their own futures, that they are 'authors of their own lives', even in the most obscure or inaccessible areas of employment or higher education.

Respondents had a range of priorities for what they would deem successful future employment, including wealth, financial security, status, realizing their parents' aspirations and, for a small number, achieving social mobility; these aspirations are discussed in chapter 5. But they all shared a belief that hard work and gaining a competitive edge were key ingredients for fulfilling their particular priorities. Molly, from the Felix Holt B group, reflected these sentiments:

> Alan Sugar started with nothing really, he came from a council estate and built his career up by himself, so that's so inspirational for me – he had a goal that he's achieved and is still achieving it; he's quite smart, knows the business, knows what needs to be done, and he's dedicated, probably got good grades.

Yet, as Toynbee argues, contemporary British society:

> is less mobile with class at birth a more certain destiny than a generation ago. People cling to the belief that merit trumps class – but the Alan Sugars and Damon Buffinis are famous because their rags to riches tales are so exceptional.
>
> (Toynbee, 2010: 29)

A further four students from the Felix Holt B group also believed that they would achieve their future goals through hard work and individual agency. Marilyn was committed to achieving a high-status career: 'I want grades to do the bar standards one-year course for barristers, after my three-year degree. I've always been interested in it, I've enjoyed it and can see myself working in that sort of environment.' Simon was less selective and wanted a job doing 'anything I can control and have a say in what happens is what I want. I don't want to be at the bottom and having no effect, I want to be able to have a say; in TV production I could have a say in how it goes.'

Darren was keen to pursue a celebrity lifestyle, to have plenty of money and the freedom that can provide. He is a committed footballer who dreams of having a successful playing career, which he intends to achieve by working hard.

Two students from South Park, one from the A group and one from the B group, said they felt they possessed the individual agency necessary to gain a senior position in their future employment. They wanted to influence high-level decision-making in their places of work. Hannah explained that she sees 'power as a goal in life; to be in a position of being at the top that can show ultimate success'. Julian told us that for him 'success is proving myself to teachers, and achieving my estimated grades, A*s, As and some Bs. I'm hoping for university or being a policeman.'

All these respondents believe in the power of their own efforts and feel that, with hard work and commitment, they will be able to achieve their goals of gaining high status employment, such as becoming a famous footballer or a barrister. In their talk of gaining status and power they are unaware that they are growing up in one of the most unequal societies in Europe (Wilkinson and Pickett, 2009). They do not acknowledge that, if they move up the career ladder, some others will potentially move down, as there are only limited economic goods available. They are hugely driven and motivated by the possibilities represented by gaining high-status occupations.

Four of the respondents at Felix Holt actively sought economic security in their futures and said they were prepared to work hard to achieve this goal. Many had experienced some kind of financial hardship in their families and this influenced their desire to seek employment security. Experiencing financial hardship had made a notable and lasting impression on these young people, who were strategizing and rationalizing about the best way to ensure that they achieved security. Many sought to move beyond the occupational status of their parents. For example, Michael discussed how his family has suffered as a result of the prolonged economic downturn:

> A few years ago we were comfortable but as the recession hit my step-dad found it hard to get work, money became tight; things we don't have now we used to have and so we have made cutbacks. But this has given me more reason to go to university to get a better job for myself; Nottingham and electronic engineering. It's not going to be easy, but it's not too hard. I feel confident about the grades.

Rachael told us that she believes her future is 'entirely in my own hands and childhood is the chance to build on family, morals and economic security, but when you leave school you start to realize you can shape your family'. Similarly, Rob told us that 'from now, the future is entirely in my own hands'. Matt told us that he wants to climb the career ladder and achieve higher social status than that enjoyed by his parents. He wants to build his career around his own company, demonstrating his entrepreneurial aspirations. A common theme for these students was the perception that their futures were in their own hands; that with hard work and commitment they could achieve their goals. They were certain they possessed the agency necessary to negotiate any structural constraints or limitations, although some of them came from families where academic underachievement has been the norm.

These are interesting examples in light of Bourdieu's (1977a) theoretical framework of habitus, field and dispositions and research into the important impact of early familial relationships. Habitus is context-specific and historically rooted, as we can see in this group of students' discussions about their dispositions to move beyond their familial habitus by pursuing particular employment aspirations. They conceived these aspirations not as a turn away from family values or a demonstration of disrespect toward their families, but as a way of securing a brighter, more prosperous and financially secure future – for themselves and ultimately their children.

In the Felix Holt B group, Tania, Dave and Paula were very aware of the additional pressure that having their own families would place on their ability to develop and sustain their employment pathways, largely because they had observed and experienced the struggles their parents had undergone. All three were willing to work hard to ensure their success. Tania told us that she would not consider having a family until her career was well established. For Dave, 'promotion and more money is very important, especially with family and children. Promotion in areas I'm interested in. I'd like to do an armed response; I don't know how you get there yet.' In some ways, this response is idealistic; Dave believed that hard work alone would ensure his success and did not acknowledge the external constraints that could influence his career.

Paula was ambitious for her future and keen to secure a professional career. She told us 'I would like to eventually become a head, not even still working for schools but moving on to do something related to schools like Ofsted rather than a simple teaching career'. She had ambitions to do a 'further degree so I'm not limited to teaching'. Paula was keen to ensure that she achieved not only a career but also transferable skills to afford her possibilities within a range of professional careers.

These B group respondents were not put off by the hard work and challenges that lay ahead in their chosen career pathways, and were confident that their agency, coupled with hard work, was the key to their futures. They talked convincingly about their commitment to their imagined prosperous futures. Whether they possessed the resilience and tenacity required to overcome career or life challenges is impossible to know; most of them did not acknowledge that their career futures could be other than what they wanted.

These plans for the future highlight the respondents' beliefs that they are being educated in a meritocracy that will reward hard work and desire. They take full responsibility for their own future choices and associated risks; in doing so the self is being reflexively made (Giddens, 1991). They are motivated and committed to achieving their upwardly mobile goals and believe that their futures are in their own hands, that they are driving their destinies and will not be influenced by any of the structural inequalities in wider society. They do not perceive that multiple axes of differentiation – social class, gender and race – will influence their ambitions and future outcomes. These expectations are contrary to much of the research conducted with young people exploring their aspirations and outcomes (see Archer *et al.*, 2010; Ball *et al.*, 2000), which show that identity and structural inequality are significant factors that influence the sort of achievements possible for particular groups of young people.

The respondents strongly reflect the rhetoric perpetuated by New Labour, where the emphasis was on an individualized, meritocratic ideal suggesting that all young people can be educationally successful and upwardly mobile if they choose to be, want it enough and are prepared to work hard to realize their dreams. Such a discourse can be read as incredibly high-risk because of the way it locates success and failure with the individual: if young people set out to achieve a certain goal but cannot reach or obtain it then, in this discourse, it must be their fault, because they have had access to the same education system as those who do succeed. There is no acknowledgement of the advantages possessed by some families in terms of social and cultural capital or privileged habitus. There is no evidence that the respondents are aware of the impact their identities will have on their future progression and employment possibilities. They feel that they simply need to select a future pathway, work hard and believe in themselves, and success in reaching their goals will be assured.

Competition

The students were asked about their views and perceptions of their academic examinations. Eight students in the South Park A group, four students in the South Park B group, two students in the Felix Holt A group and two students in the Felix Holt B group said they were highly competitive in their examinations and other areas of their school life, including sport. This is not particularly surprising in the current context, with the growing credentialization of the labour market and greater aspirations for increased participation in higher education (Barker, 2012). The students seem to have internalized these governmental policies and, as chapter 4 shows, in many cases their ambitions were positively reinforced by their parents and the schools.

Being competitive was cited as an aspect of success most frequently by respondents in the South Park A group, with eight students reporting this as a source of motivation for their school success. The areas of competition identified included academic examinations, sporting achievements and participation in extracurricular activities. These respondents enjoyed the thrill and buzz of being competitive and told us they thrived on the challenge. For example, Sean is motivated by examination success and he told us: 'I'm excited by good grades back from an exam. I think they are a measure of my success in general.' Noah felt it was important to be competitive, not just in his academic work but also in his various sporting endeavours. He explained that for him 'it's all about sport, about competing and competitiveness, this is what excites me'. Asked what he considered success to be, Oliver explained that 'trying to win is an achievement ... and success is also about getting that far in the competition and you want to do yourself justice'. Jacob told us he is 'highly competitive in everything I do, but I just can't help it, blame Monopoly, I've always got to win'. Isabella said that for her, success 'would be winning to get to the top of a profession, just getting into medicine is competitive'.

Sebastian (South Park B group) saw doing well in examinations as an important marker of his school success, and said he was very competitive in many areas of his schooling. Alison told us that competition motivated her and pushed her to do better. She welcomed the opportunity to develop and improve her academic work, and said examination competition was one way for her to achieve this goal.

Peer competition

In the South Park A and B groups, peer competition was cited as a key aspect of being competitive. It is not enough for these respondents to be successful against their own individualized goals and criteria. Peer competition was cited as a significant motivational factor that pushed these respondents to avoid complacency in their academic studies.

For instance, in the South Park A group, four of the eight respondents who enjoyed competition also thrived on competing with their peers. Ellie said that:

> If you allow yourself to stop working then you have a problem because part of it (success) is comparing yourself with other people. I look at what other people have got, and I often conclude they're rubbish and so competitiveness is a huge driver for me especially as we get towards exams.

Owen explained in some detail his desire to compete and outdo his peers:

> Rather if you've done well, and done better than other people ... I don't feel I've had a great achievement unless I've worked hard for it. I'm competitive and I always would like to do better than others ... Doing better than others is more important than just doing well in motivating me.

Clare told us that success was competing and 'doing better than other people'. Elijah observed a culture of competitiveness in the school and reported that, although he and his friends got on well, they were very competitive with each other in all areas of their schooling and this 'drives the success forwards and prevents complacency'.

In the South Park B group two of the four students who enjoyed competition similarly reported their enjoyment in terms of peer competition. Jasmine was motivated by competing with her peers and said she feels better when she achieves higher examination results than her friends. Sharon also enjoyed competing with her peers and, although she said she was pleased when they achieved, she was also keen to succeed academically herself.

These respondents are unafraid of competing against their friends in order to secure their own advantage. They cannot afford to reduce their academic efforts; there is no space to sit back on their laurels. Rather they need to continually prove themselves through examination success in hyper-performative times. But it is interesting that their narratives convey a sense of ease with these demands – they are not put off by the pressure but motivated and engaged by it. Their talk about competition chimes with Gove's desire for everyone to become the 'authors of their own life stories', freed from any external or structural constraints and taking full responsibility for their own actions and outcomes (DfE, 2010a: 6).

In Bourdieu's (1993a) terms it seems that these students' habitus and dispositions are aligned to the formal demands and expectations of the school, and that the students are comfortable with what is demanded of them. This is not surprising, as they are attending a very good school that has a sizeable middle-class intake and ambitious, enabling and aspirant teachers. They understand the importance of competition and examination success in an education system that emphasizes narrow, results-based, target-driven outcomes. Even the students who said they were not particularly motivated by examination success (Anna, Sandy and Gavin) acknowledged the importance of achieving formal academic qualifications if they wanted to progress and obtain paid employment.

The respondents at Felix Holt School talked far less about a preoccupation with competitive examination success, reflecting perhaps the subtle yet notable differences within the student body. Felix Holt is widely respected as a very good school, but it has a more diverse social class intake than South Park and this is evident in the students' aspirations. Across the group of 42 students, only four explicitly expressed a desire for success in examinations or other forms of competition such as sport, compared with twelve students at South Park. Of these, two were in the A group and two in the B group.

But in contrast to South Park, the students at Felix Holt who did desire success did not see competing with their peers as an important part of that success, though they were keen to compete with siblings or to achieve against their individualized goals. For example, in the A group, Colin felt that competing to be successful in sport was important: 'the main influence would be sport; it influences how I interact with people. I play hockey now, but I used to play other sports. It's mainly an expression of competitiveness; I need to get it out of my system.' For Jack, also in the A group, being successful meant achieving more than his siblings: 'I have three siblings, I'm the second oldest, so there is a lot of drive to compete against them. My older brother got 3 As and a D, I want to beat him; he did Maths at Leicester.' These examples of a desire for competition could be read as gendered identity productions as they reflect a hegemonic construction of masculinity (Connell, 2005), as evident in Colin's assertion that he needs to compete in sport to get the competitiveness out of his system. Jack needs to compete against his brother's seemingly effortless and authentic academic achievement and beat his 3 As.

In the Felix Holt B group, Emilio explained that he is 'quite competitive, and it's important to try to win'. Molly told us that she is 'hoping to go into trading, on the stock market; I do economics ... I'm very competitive'. These respondents expressed a desire to compete on their own terms in relation to their individualized targets and goals. Perhaps this is partly because the institutional habitus of the school was subtly different to that of South Park and placed more emphasis on the attainment of individual targets rather than success through a competitive, league-type approach.

These respondents' desire for examination competition and other forms of success resonates with a wider discourse identified by Giddens (1991), who documented latent individualization amongst persons, particularly youth, as they seek to further their own opportunities, often at the expense of, or in competition with, their peers. The respondents' comments reflect their sentiments around individualized ambition and draw attention to a shift in their aspirations. The students' comments about their desire for examination success demonstrate that they have internalized discourses about the importance of gaining formal qualifications. They buy into the possibilities offered by individualization, where individual success is the primary concern, rather than community engagement and the satisfaction of striving for shared goals and achievements. They reflect a strategic, neo-liberal subjectivity that emphasizes the rights and priorities of the individual but is less concerned with the rights and priorities of a group.

These respondents have internalized the language of grades, targets and performance to a remarkable degree and they are committed to achieving the best possible results. They talked expertly about their chances of improving in weaker subjects, and of the need to revise effectively to secure a good grade. They believe that the school represents a meritocracy and believe that hard work will be rewarded. Not surprisingly, several of them reported that examination success excited and motivated them, but only if they achieved results that satisfied them.

Getting ahead?

This chapter has shown that the majority of our respondents believed the meritocratic school ideal that hard work will always be rewarded. The rewards might consist of achieving a coveted place at an elite university, accessing one of the few high-status vocational pathways to gaining a qualification, or gaining desirable forms of employment. Several of the respondents in both schools were highly competitive and motivated by competing against their peers in formal examinations and other areas, including sport. They understood the qualifications game and were at ease with the demands it placed on them. Most were experts on the subject of their own achievement and were able to identify areas for improvement and describe the benefits of targeted revision in this process. They were generally objective and rational in their talk about how to achieve in the education system, and almost all were confident in their ability to negotiate the system and to use it to maximize their potential and realize their aspirations. In this way, the respondents can be constructed as reflexive agents of individualism, keenly aware of the way that the examination system rewards hard work and confident of the promise of the meritocratic ideal.

The chapter has also examined the respondents' optimistic plans for their futures and their unwavering belief in their own efforts, hard work and thus personal agency as a means to achieve future economic security and, in many cases, to experience for themselves the same level of social mobility enjoyed by their parents and grandparents. The dominant view reflected an idealized version of education, where one must simply work hard and choose the right courses and places to study in order to secure the future. They also seem naive in their talk about future plans, displaying little understanding of the complex processes that can affect future success, for example, structural inequality in wider society. They viewed their embodied selves with neutrality and were unwilling to acknowledge the limitations that some aspects of identity may place on their future prospects.

Yet the respondents' dispositions to choose particular pathways are circumscribed by their identities. For example, students whose parents had professional careers as, for example, doctors, lawyers and professors, were greatly influenced by this high-status and academic milieu experienced from childhood. Similarly, those students whose parents had experienced more vocationally oriented careers as, for example, plumbers, builders and hairdressers, were likely to aspire to similar forms of occupational employment. Thus, social mobility for our sample could be constrained by the respondents' habitus and dispositions, which in turn meant that the dominant social class model we encountered was one of reproduction through the education system, although with some notable gender exceptions, which are discussed in chapter 6.

What does this picture tell us about the prospects of social mobility for students in our two high-status, ambitious and Ofsted-praised schools? Perhaps the most striking point is the evidence that government rhetoric about the importance of gaining academic qualifications is the dominant discourse in both schools and is emphasized as a key component of the students' future success. The students have absorbed and internalized discourses about examination success holding the key to their futures and were strategic, objective and rational about their pathways and choices. Teachers were important in securing their students' success through the accreditation system, and encouraged them to pursue further and higher academic qualifications. The students' dreams centred on securing the necessary qualifications to enter their chosen (frequently high-status) professions, scarcely acknowledging that they might fail to achieve their goals.

A final important point relates to the changing labour market. The ever-increasing credentialization of the labour market over the past 25 years has meant that many of the respondents intend to pursue degrees to enter forms of employment that have become subject to greater regulation and accreditation requirements. Many jobs that did not require a degree in the 1980s, particularly in clerical and administrative areas of employment, now do. Whilst a number of our respondents may be going further in the post-compulsory education market than their parents, in terms of mobility they are often running in order to stand still (Brown, 2001).

We encountered overwhelmingly strategic, astute, highly motivated and hard-working students who were agents of individualism, supported by their teachers and parents in their attempts to secure future economic stability and status. But what might their prospects really be?

Chapter 4
Families and children

Introduction

South Park and Felix Holt are state-of-the-art academies, prototypes for a new generation of schooling, and our findings (chapter 3) illustrate their success in producing a culture and practice that has enhanced opportunity, quality and performance. The Coalition believes the new academy regime, generalized across the country, will overcome family circumstances that narrow life chances for too many young people and that imprint patterns of inequality from one generation to the next (HMG, 2011: 3). The academy concept embodies the promise that every child can be the author of their own lives, unconstrained by the narrowing influence of their family's work, resources and expectations.

The claim that effective schools overcome family disadvantage is contradicted, however, by a number of studies primarily concerned with examination results. As we saw in chapter 2, poverty seems to exert a consistently stronger influence than teachers, schools and education, even when extensive support has been provided to improve social inclusion (Mortimore and Whitty, 2000; Raffo, 2011). Interventions designed to help disadvantaged working-class families to emulate middle-class attitudes and behaviour have achieved little (Gewirtz, 2001). The relatively poor performance of children in receipt of FSMs has not improved over time (see Table 2.1, p. 21), although schools have devoted great energy to 'closing the gap' (HMG, 2011; Cook, 2012).

This evidence of the persistent failure to overcome disadvantage, despite substantial public investment in areas with high concentrations of disadvantaged people, and the alternative perspectives reviewed in chapter 2, lead us to adopt a different approach to investigating the connection between family background and education. We believe the relationship between wealth and school performance is linear and graduated, not polarized between the virtuous middle class and the urban disadvantaged. The use of the FSM indicator to identify a group of less-well-off people that can be compared with the population at large has generated the misleading impression of a performance gap between the least advantaged and the rest. This has led policy-makers to concentrate on 'closing the gap' rather than worrying about the steady decline in performance across the income spectrum.

Policy thus aims to reduce outcome differences between social groups and between schools, but has failed to consider other factors that may explain why gradations in income are closely associated with gradations in student performance at the vast majority of schools. Family background and circumstances are presented as obstacles to be overcome, rather than as significant influences on young people's attitudes and behaviour that should be investigated and understood (HMG, 2011: 3). Governments expect us to disregard the complex social and cultural processes involved in social mobility, and to concentrate instead on perceived weaknesses in the education system, as if they were the cause of relative poverty and its consequences.

This chapter investigates families and children from a different perspective. We regard the family as vitally important for the child's development, not as an obstacle that blights the prospects of an unfortunate minority. Our interviews enabled us to explore how family experiences have influenced young people's personal development, as well as their choices of educational and employment pathways. We draw on Bourdieu's concept of habitus to make sense of the 'durable dispositions' acquired by our respondents through their family socialization, and to examine the ways in which family resources are transmitted between generations. We recognize the tension between the students' agency and the societal structures that constrain them but emphasize their 'practical sense' and scope for personal action (Bourdieu, 1977a; 1993a).

Our data shows that families are a potent and formative influence in young people's lives and that their role needs to be understood before we can hope to explain the relationship between relative wealth, education and social mobility. We challenge the idea that schools can in some way 'overcome' the family experiences that shape the way people are, and, through the students' stories, present evidence that parents, siblings and other significant relatives work to produce social stability rather than change or transformation. There is little sign that South Park and Felix Holt have overcome family influences or reduced the effects of relative poverty.

Supportive families

Within the environments provided by the two schools, students perceived themselves to be well supported and encouraged by very helpful parents and families. Over 70 per cent of respondents cited particular examples of their parents supporting and helping them. Hannah perceived her parents as playing a vital role in her self-organization and progress:

> My parents are very encouraging in terms of prompting me,
> getting me to places on time, encouraging me to organize; my Dad
> is always trying to advise me, always trying to do what's best for
> me in my school work, helping with projects.

Oliver said his parents have 'strived to make me achieve the best I can' while Mark said that his parents motivated him to revise and made sure he did things. Samantha said her parents had always encouraged her to work hard at school, while Sharon was eager to please 'my mum and dad' who 'push me to do really well'. Parents were also reported (in interviews with Lance, Rebecca, Rachael, Mary, and Tom) to have helped with extracurricular activities, trips and work experience. Several respondents (Layla, Gemma, and Tania) recognized the importance of their parents' high expectations.

Students most frequently cited the importance of happy relationships at home and the encouraging nature of their parents' contribution. Jack said he had a good relationship with both parents that 'makes me feel relaxed at home and allows me to do work'. Jordan explained that his mother was 'behind me the whole time, encouraging me, helping me at home'. Rebecca found her mother's encouragement 'really good'. Patrick's family had 'always been there to help me through stuff' while Carl particularly appreciated the good backing he receives from his family, while emphasizing that success is ultimately 'down to me and the effort I put in'.

Although none of the respondents seemed dissatisfied with the help and support they received, there were occasional criticisms of one or other parent, especially in the case of divorce or separation. Alice, for example, said that her main sustenance came from her mother:

> I'm trying to prove my dad wrong because he thinks I'm a waste
> of space. I'm trying to prove I'm fine, he wants me running back
> to him, he left me as a child, I've grown up with my mum. It's
> made me more independent and more determined. My mum has
> motivated me to carry on with what I want to do; she's the one
> who has given me the support I need.

Other students emphasized the positive contributions of their fathers. Harry said his Dad had 'always been there for me, I look up to him a lot, he's always given me his full support', while Tony reported that his father had encouraged him to go to university when 'my mum didn't want me to go'. But most students in both schools agreed that they needed support and encouragement, and resisted overt pushing. Faith appreciated the fact that her parents 'don't push, they know what I can do, they know what I can get and see no point in pushing harder'. Mark saw himself as very fortunate because 'my family gives me lots of support behind whatever I do, so I don't feel pressured to do things'.

Overall, the interviews provide strong evidence that students and parents at South Park and Felix Holt shared common aspirations and goals, and collaborated effectively with one another to secure the best possible examination grades. The students reported a close alignment between their families and schools in the pursuit of high-quality educational outcomes, with only Sandy and Gavin at South Park expressing dissatisfaction with their school's aims and values. Other less-capable students, like Patrick, said they were working hard to achieve good grades, and appreciated the school's sustained effort to help them.

Advantaged, disadvantaged

Few students believed they were hindered by disadvantage, poverty or lack of resources, and most tended to interpret less positive circumstances as challenges to be overcome, rather than as explanations for lower levels of academic success. Respondents self-identified as follows:

Table 4.1: Student self-identification of family economic background

Term used	16+ A group	16+ B group	18+ A group	18+ B group
Advantaged/ privileged	11	4	6	6
Average	9	6	7	5
Disadvantaged	0	3	1	0
Family problems	1	4	2	5
No reference	3	5	2	8

Within this generally positive picture, where students feel well supported and strongly positioned to progress in their education and careers, there is evidence of significant variation in the economic pressure experienced at the two schools, and by those included in the A and B groups at South Park. A number of individuals, particularly those placed in the B groups, described difficult personal and economic situations that seemed to be affecting their educational and career trajectories in a variety of unacknowledged ways.

South Park A group

The family culture and backgrounds described are remarkably similar within the group, with a notable concentration of parents with academic, professional, scientific and technical expertise. An unusual number occupy positions as leading academics (including several professors at prestigious universities), scientific researchers and teachers. Research and development predominates, even amongst those working in the private sector. Respondents' parents in general are well educated, with a significant proportion holding PhD and high-level professional qualifications.

A small majority of the A group described themselves as advantaged. Rose pointed out that although she is now 'reasonably advantaged', her family was poor when she was growing up, because her parents had children young and 'had no money'. She is grateful for her good fortune and doesn't 'take things for granted'. Sean said he is advantaged because both his parents are professors, while Jacob felt 'privileged because we have a nice house' and the 'financial crash hasn't affected us'. Students who identified themselves as coming from 'average' backgrounds were more cautious. Sophie considered that her 'family is about average; we don't have masses of money but are not exactly poor'. Owen 'never considered myself disadvantaged in any way' while Mark judged that 'we're not rich but have enough'. No student thought themselves to be disadvantaged, under-privileged or poor. Only one student reported a family problem.

South Park B group

A majority of the B group believed they were average or disadvantaged, and there were numerous references to financial pressure, family break-up and other difficulties arising from illness or disability. Occupational backgrounds were mainly related to the local economy (e.g. hairdresser, decorator, cleaner) and often included periods of unemployment. Max related that his parents were 'living in a squat when I was born' and said the family has 'never really had much money'. Anna admitted that 'we're quite disadvantaged, we don't get as much money as others, it affects going on school trips and things'. Leah felt her family was quite disadvantaged. Sharon disclosed that her parents had been 'at the bottom' and 'have gained their way to a comfortable living' by hard work.

A number of personal and family problems were cited, invariably as examples of issues to be overcome, but there were references to emotional disturbances that might hamper the student's concentration on academic work. Freddie, for example, said he was suffering because his parents do not live together and admitted he was much less positive about life than he would like to be. He was considering a professional cookery diploma as a career route. Alison reported that her parents parted about nine months before the interview and there was a period 'when I felt really distracted; when conversations came up I'd be upset in a lesson'.

Felix Holt A and B groups

Student backgrounds at Felix Holt are more diverse than at South Park, but have common roots in a prosperous local economy that grew strongly in the post-war period, and between the mid-1990s and 2008. A mix of skilled and unskilled manual occupations predominate in the older industrial districts of the area, while the owners of local businesses, London commuters, white collar employees and self-employed tradesmen tend to inhabit neighbouring suburban and village locations.

Few of those interviewed referred to professional, academic or high-level technical employment backgrounds. Many students reported that their families have suffered economic hardship since 2008, with their insecurity reflecting marked fluctuations in the local labour market. Even respondents who said they came from advantaged homes referred to uncertainty and changes in prosperity over time, mainly due to broken relationships and discontinuities of employment.

A minority of Felix Holt students deemed themselves to be advantaged. Charlotte considered that she has been 'quite lucky' but pointed out that her parents were not well off when they grew up, and even now were not especially well paid. Jack said his family was probably 'a little above average in that [his] parents have well-paid jobs' but explained his mother worked only part time and his father's wages have to be 'shared out amongst four children'. Gemma was appreciative of the advantages she enjoyed but also reported that her father had been made redundant, so could no longer afford to send her on trips around the world, a privilege that other candidates she met at her interview at a prestigious university still enjoyed.

Rachael felt 'quite privileged in terms of things I get from my parents'. Tania said she and her brother were lucky without realizing 'how lucky we are, our parents have provided well'. Emilio said that his family 'is advantaged' but pointed out the importance of women's earnings: 'In my family my mother is definitely the breadwinner, my dad does a job, not a good job, but it is hard to get a job in this economic climate'. Lucy admitted that her family were living on their savings after her father's redundancy and his subsequent inability to find stable and suitable work.

A majority of Felix Holt students described themselves as 'average' but also mentioned a variety of domestic pressures. Andrew said that he was living in a tight financial situation, while Michael noted that 'as the recession hit, my stepdad found it hard to get work and money became tight and there have been cutbacks'. Holly felt that 'we're comfortable at the moment but we're living on savings rather than current income'. Her mother's business had kept the family afloat since her father's redundancy eighteen months earlier. Others stressed the extent to which they have been supported personally despite financial pressure. Graham said: 'My parents have provided everything I need, I've had no disadvantage but no huge advantage, they don't spoil me with unnecessary things, they've been good.' Nick considered himself to be part of an 'average family' where there was enough money 'for me to do what I want'.

B group students at Felix Holt were much more likely to cite personal experiences of separation and divorce, and also to acknowledge the ways in which family breakdown may compound financial difficulty. Darren's father left when he was two days old, so 'my knowledge of his background is minimal, I'm not even sure of his country of origin'. Simon spent a lot of time travelling between his father in London and his mother who lives near the school, while Joyce referred to her parents' divorce and being brought up by her mother over the last ten years. She felt that divorce and financial difficulties have brought them 'down in the world'.

Despite economic hardship, personal difficulties and family problems, all those interviewed at both schools were immensely optimistic and positive about their opportunities and prospects. Adele's interview illustrates the way in which the students expected to overcome adversity. She comes from a working-class family, her parents are divorced, and she has a disabled sister, but she is determined to enter a profession that has been perceived as male-dominated. She regards disadvantages as challenges 'that enable you to develop coping strategies'. She is inspired by the example of her 'absolutely amazing' mother, who has had to go through much in life. Her mother has been 'the only constant' in her upbringing, communicating a strong set of family values as well as a sense of stability and security.

This data seems to confirm the government's belief that good and outstanding schools can make 'life chances more equal at critical points for social mobility' – for some students (HMG, 2011: 6).

Family influences

School effectiveness studies, inspection reports and performance tables have added to the widespread perception that places like Felix Holt and South Park are models of excellence that should be followed across the country, offering a ladder of opportunity to everyone (Sammons *et al.*, 1995; Adonis,

2012). Our participants' views of their personal constraints seem to confirm that classroom excellence can be emulated everywhere, with important consequences for social mobility and change. This may encourage policy-makers to feel confident about education's transformative power and to deny strongly the idea that schools reproduce the social order. Such policy-makers tend to disregard the alternative thesis that students' learning is structured by dispositions arising from their families and the conditions of their lives and experience (Adonis, 2012; Bourdieu and Passeron, 1977; Bourdieu, 1990).

Our interviews were designed, therefore, to elicit information and perceptions relating to respondents' families. Their stories, explored below, show the strong and pervasive influence of parents and social background, even when students appear to be exercising a strong personal agency, with mum and dad apparently in the background. The data provides evidence of how family culture and dynamics have contributed to students' emerging identities and dispositions, with the children progressively positioning themselves in relation to behaviour and models provided by grandparents, parents and siblings, as well as absorbing implicit and explicit values and priorities. Parents appear to be deeply invested in their children's education and future success, as well as important sources of interests and hobbies.

Resources and identity

The data on students' economic circumstances (Appendices 1 and 2) shows a considerable range of experience at both schools, with degrees of ill health, separation, divorce and unemployment limiting the resources available for some, while others have enjoyed sustained prosperity, usually based on a mix of full- and part-time parental incomes. As we have seen, respondents were inclined to describe 'advantage' in modest terms and to discount the negatives usually associated with below-average incomes. Although they acknowledged the significance of family histories, they portrayed themselves as active participants and their interviews reflected interpretations and responses as varied as the individuals and conditions described.

Parental occupations were often reported as a significant influence on respondents' growing sense of personal identity and status. Elijah (A group, South Park) described how his parents' work and income had opened unusual opportunities with great significance for his own international academic aspirations and outlook. His father, from Australia, is a professor at a top university, while his mother, from Germany, is a leading cancer researcher. Sean's (A group, South Park) parents are both university professors and this seems to have shaped his desire to operate 'at a high level, in a lot of detail'. Like Elijah, he has an international perspective and regards Canada as a 'good bet' for higher education. He wouldn't want to be 'something like a teacher'. Clare, (A group, South Park), who also saw herself as financially advantaged, had a different opinion about teaching, expressing a desire to join the profession and work with children, an ambition that she linked directly with her mother's occupation as a teacher. She argued that 'if you are more advantaged in terms of money, you feel you are more able' and that less fortunate people 'feel there's no point'.

Other students who self-identified as 'advantaged' also tended to regard themselves as intelligent and capable, often displaying great confidence in talking about course options and future careers. Tania (B group, Felix Holt) was amongst 30 or so students in her cohort who had transferred to the sixth form at Felix Holt after GCSE. She had switched because her previous school was small; she wanted to escape the 'bubble' and meet new people. She had arrived with an expectation of success, and was head girl at the time of her interview, but was struggling to achieve the grades required for veterinary college despite her good GCSE results and undoubted linguistic and social skills:

> My family are middle, perhaps upper-middle class, we're well off … there was a time when my brother and I were both at private schools and my dad worked hard for that, we're fairly well spoken, they've taught us manners, we help around the house and we're lucky and don't realize how lucky we are, our parents have provided well for me. They want me to go ahead … My future is 100 per cent down to how I perform in the next couple of weeks.

Less-advantaged but highly-rated students (i.e. those predicted to attain A* grades) tended to identify with a parent or parents who had shown skill and determination in overcoming financial difficulties. Andrew (A group, Felix Holt) said that his lone-parent mother had 'enabled him to spend thousands on cameras, despite '"harder-than-most" financial circumstances'. He aligned himself with her skills and work ethic. Lucy (A group, South Park) was plainly discouraged by her father's spells of unemployment and reduced status. Before the recession he had been a printer with a local council, but he was made redundant in the first wave of cuts. Since then he had been in and out of work, losing another job and resorting to 'bad agency work that lasted one day'. She was acutely aware that 'you don't get bigger presents at Christmas' and her sister has had to give up horse riding. But Lucy identified with her hardworking mother, who refused absolutely to allow her father to give up. Fortunately her mum is 'good with money', so the family had been able to fall back on investments and savings.

The recession had influenced other Felix Holt A group students, including Ben. His car salesman father has been made redundant and his mother has been compelled to return to work. He was unusual in questioning whether future success could come from hard work and qualifications alone. He argued that if you want to be a teacher when there are cuts to public sector jobs, 'it is going to be an issue when you look for work'. He acknowledged 'deep social barriers' in our society and wondered if businessmen like Richard Branson would be so successful if they were born in a poor part of South Africa. 'With business', he claimed, 'you need money in the first place'; he felt quite strongly that inherited fortunes are unfair. Ben's pessimism was grounded in his family's recent experience and informed his cautious approach to career options and his willingness to adopt a critical outlook.

Our data suggests that illness and poverty are not incidental misfortunes but formative ingredients in family histories that have long-term effects on young people's personal development, self-perceptions and life chances. Anna (B group, South Park), for example, came from a large, disadvantaged family that had been unable to pay for school trips, fashionable clothes or even materials for GCSE art. She had helped a lot with her brothers and sisters at home and her family role had led to work experience at a nursery. Anna's family believed childcare was a good career option for her because she was good with her younger siblings. Her sisters had told her what to expect and she was confident she would enjoy working with children. Her parents supported her education and 'talk to me as much as possible to make sure I understand everything'. She reported that she is on target for a vocational course at a further education college.

Leah (B group, South Park) presented as an able student, expected to achieve B grades at GCSE, but it soon emerged that struggles with traumatic family issues had disrupted her life and compromised her education. Her brother had heart disease, a situation that had affected everyone in the family because he needed continuous care. Her father was unable to work due to illness, and her mother had never been able to work because of her son's problems. Income was 'a slight problem'. There were four children in all, each with a 'big deal problem'. Leah reported problems with depression and hard work at school. She said she had missed lots of lessons because she was reluctant to do the things the school was doing at the time and because 'I didn't feel it was what I wanted to do'. She claimed that the situation has made her very independent: 'I like to do what I think is right and the way to be'.

Young people's identities and aspirations are related to family resources, dispositions and habitus as well as their perceptions of parental status and engagement with the wider community (Bourdieu, 1977a). Some respondents also identified strongly with proactive parents who have overcome difficulties through hard work or by mobilizing available skills and networks. Our interviews indicate that ill health, unstable families and reduced incomes should not necessarily be seen as short-term misfortunes but as enduring conditions that may shape family history and influence individual identities. As in the case of Leah, such difficulties may also constrain ambition and lead family members to accept low-status options. Even relatively brief experiences of reduced income and status can induce caution, anxiety and pessimism in the wider family, as in the case of Ben.

Family role models

Participants consistently described one or both parents as an important influence on their own long-term behaviour and dispositions. The interview data suggested that students draw to a high degree on family role models. Andrew (A group, Felix Holt) shared his mother's belief that 'if you want to be somewhere you have to work to get there' and recognized a strong connection between his own desire to be a wildlife photographer and her talent as an artist-illustrator. Rob (A group, Felix Holt) acknowledged the extent to which his own instincts derived from his mother:

> My mum taught me to be an individual and never pushed me to do homework. I took the initiative to do it myself because I've never had that pressure, apart from occasional nudges when younger. When I asked for help, I got it ... from now on the future is entirely in my own hands. Your parents give you basic rules and expectations that are hard to change and set your identity but now it's all down to me.

Elijah (A group, South Park) described his parents' roles in enhancing his knowledge and opportunities. He had accompanied his father on consultancy work overseas and had developed an international perspective on the future. He was interested in world affairs and wanted a high-level technical job, perhaps in economics, aeronautical engineering or international relations. His parents had supported him in every way, providing extra tuition in mathematics, because he had found the lessons too easy at that time, and in German, to help him to take the examination two years early. They were 'prepared to spend what it takes to help me do well'.

Some parents were described as having adopted child-rearing practices diametrically opposed to those they experienced themselves. Ellie (A group, South Park), for example, had never been pushed or pressurized because her mother was driven to do well at a private boarding school, only to discover that when she left and the pressure was off she stopped bothering. Her father had a similar experience. He was entered for A-level English early and got into Oxford to study law but did not enjoy it and left, eventually becoming a drama teacher. This family history seems to have made Ellie doubtful about pursuing material success and advancement. Although she was predicted to obtain a full set of A* GCSE grades, she said that 'success for me would be making people happy and feeling happy myself'.

In some cases, misfortune prompted the next generation to teach their offspring the need for financial independence and security. Julian (B group, South Park) said that his father, who worked as a mathematics teacher, encouraged him to be as independent as possible, mainly because his own father left him when he was small: he had bought his son a paper round business to run. Julian employed two people and was 'making a lot of money and paying my dad back'. He claimed he had become 'a greedy person ... motivated a lot' by money, although he said he never judged people on money. The experience had not encouraged him to pursue an entrepreneurial career, however. From a young age he had wanted to be a policeman, like his maternal grandfather. He explained that he liked the idea of 'serving the community' and 'working up the ranks to higher status'. Julian's dispositions acted as boundaries, setting the limits of his class habitus, and thus served as 'broad parameters and boundaries of what is possible or unlikely for a particular group in a stratified social world' (Swartz, 1997: 103).

Sebastian (B group, South Park) reported that he was dyslexic and predicted to achieve D or E grades at GCSE, despite his engaging personality and apparent intelligence. He was strongly supported by his relatively wealthy and supportive family, however. Their outlook, guidance and direct intervention had shaped his schooling and aspirations in positive ways. In response to educational issues, Sebastian's parents decided to move both their sons from London to South Park, a school within commuting distance of their business commitments in town. He explained that:

> My whole family is pushing me to do what I want to do; they've all supported me. My friends and family are behind me. My mum says she'll support me with resources etc. and thinks veterinary nurse will be a good job, or even radio.

Now Sebastian was headed towards further education and a diploma, in veterinary nursing or animal care.

Max's (B group, South Park) family have experienced poverty and homelessness, shaping the outlook and priorities they have transmitted.

Although Max claimed that he was 'a completely different person' from his father, he was 'entirely grateful' that he had learned a lot from a difficult life and had been brought up to live off the fruits of his own labour on the family vegetable patch. Max expressed admiration for his father's lack of interest in money and was critical of the media's portrayal of success as being about money and material things. He commented that 'success is a personal thing' and argued that an 'easy life is not a good one'. His father 'never really saw the point of money' and had 'loved living on the bare minimum'. Max himself was considering a variety of creativity-based career options.

These stories show our respondents as acute observers of their parents, consciously and unconsciously learning from available examples and models, and adopting, emulating or rejecting the hallmark attitudes (e.g. to risk, insecurity, money), attributes (e.g. energy, generosity) and behaviours (e.g. child-rearing practices) that create the climate of their youth.

Family values and culture

Our participants very often began by acknowledging parental models like these but then continued to explain the pervasive influence of the values, climate and culture transmitted through their families. We interpreted the phrase 'family values' to denote values related to behaviour, aspirations and outcomes. Mia (B group, Felix Holt), for example, was aware that she acts 'a lot like my parents; [I] talk like them, believe in the things they do. I'm an atheist because my mum is.' She was expected to achieve high grades and expressed hopes of studying history at a pre-1992 university. Jason (A group, South Park) emphasized his Quaker background and said he tried to abide by the basic principles that he had taken from it. Values like equality, trust, integrity and truth were important for him. He portrayed himself as creative, enjoying art and making things that work or 'look nice', and as someone who liked having an idea and seeing it evolve into something.

Jacob (A group, South Park) was very conscious of his parents' influence, and argued that without strong values at home many students just opt out:

> Hundreds of assemblies tell you things ... we've had a lot encouraging us to improve our grades and telling us what you need to do to be successful but I'm pretty sure that most people have views on that from their parents.

Jacob's own parents had stable jobs in science and promoted reading, took a keen interest in current affairs and encouraged an awareness of the world around them, creating a secure platform for Jacob's future.

Rose (A group, South Park) was particularly appreciative of the values and culture espoused by her parents. Her father was a PhD chemist who was researching cancer cures, while her mother was a teacher of philosophy and ethics. They never put pressure on her 'because they know I'll do it for myself' but from a young age treated her as an adult and involved her as an equal in 'intelligent conversations around the dinner table'. She had dreams of travelling in space or 'perhaps going to the North Pole'. She was aiming for a top sixth form college, and then a prestigious university to study sciences. Rose liked the idea of a PhD because she had always loved 'academia, knowledge and learning, especially in scientific research'. She remarked that 'money doesn't motivate me' and said she was not 'looking for fame' but was determined that her life should be 'amazing, memorable'.

Faith (A group, South Park) told us her parents had moulded her 'by following important values needed to succeed in life', like equality and politeness. She got involved in the local youth drama group through her father's influence, so theatre productions and singing 'were there from an early age'. She loved performing, especially when singing, dancing and acting come together. This interest prompted her to choose drama, music and dance for GCSE and she had opted for performance studies at A level. She had also 'picked subjects that show I am academic' and envisaged taking a university degree in the performing arts, followed by a career as a drama teacher, with opportunities for part-time acting.

Martin (A group, Felix Holt) came from a Chinese immigrant background, and arrived at the reception stage with no English. At the time of interview he had applied to study English literature at a Russell Group university. His thoughtful responses indicated the deep influence of a complex blend of Chinese and western cultural assumptions and ideas. His father came from Hong Kong and runs a food business; his mother was from Malaysia and worked as a waitress. Martin explained that although his parents placed a high value on education, they applied no pressure. Instead, they treated him as knowing more about it than them and allowed him 'the freedom to be what I want to be'. He acknowledged that he was a 'workaholic', poised between a 'transcendental, Buddhist view of success as happiness; and the American dream of money and wealth, with five acres and a pool'.

Zara (B group, Felix Holt) said she was applying to study economics at a pre-1992 university, and hoped for a career in business. She was strongly influenced by her mother's ethos of hard work and by her uncle's success in establishing several businesses before the age of thirty. She had 'a few ideas for my own business, perhaps a cake shop or selling jewellery'. But she hadn't yet begun to think about how to acquire the necessary capital.

Some respondents acknowledged the influence of siblings in shaping their attitudes and plans. Holly (B group, Felix Holt), for example, told us she needed to achieve three C grades at A level to study animal biology at a post-1992 university. She would eventually have liked a job in the zoo industry. Her older sisters had been a major influence on her thinking: both were in careers they loved and had received promotions that had made them more comfortable in their lives. One worked in children's homes with 'disabled kids that parents can't deal with' and the other was a drugs counsellor in a high-security prison.

Lily (A group, South Park) came from a very academic family and told us how her parents and sisters had responded to her less high-powered aspirations. Her father was a well-known professor at a top university and she had two sisters studying at Oxford. She felt she had to 'live up to their standards' and was frustrated that her younger sister tended to understand 'before me'. There was a lot of family discussion about 'university stuff' but Lily remained 'pretty confident I want to work with SEN'. She had a 'strong caring side', had grown up with people who had special needs, and had done work experience in a special school. Her family was supportive but encouraged her to keep her options open. She was considering teacher training and a further degree in psychology as a possible route forward.

Some respondents reported that family experiences had made them cautious, or described their parents as risk-averse. Tom's family had been hit hard by the recession, for example. His father had been made redundant, while his mother had difficulties at work. Tom (A group, Felix Holt) said he now appreciated the middle-class privilege he enjoyed when growing up, and questioned whether the university route today leads to a guaranteed job as it once did. He didn't want 'to take a course just because other people are doing it' and felt he could have a head start on a job 'if I go out three years sooner than other people'.

Charlotte (A group, Felix Holt) said that her parents were cautious, inclined to hold back and not take risks. She said that until recently their attitude had influenced her to think in terms of a safe career as a primary school teacher. But she had reviewed things and now aimed to take a risk and become a drama teacher: 'Why not take the risk, do something I'll enjoy rather than doing something safe that would be OK but not the best thing for me?'

These student reflections capture some of the diverse and rich experiences of family life through which values and culture are transmitted. Respondents describe how they were raised, fondly remembering parents who encouraged reading, intelligent dinner table conversation, or an interest in the wider world. They praise the care and support provided by loving families and resist pressure towards an absent parent's goals. They reflect and sometimes echo their mothers' and fathers' values and commitments, learning more from family behaviour than explicit teaching or instruction. They embrace family traditions, interests and activities, quickly learning the literal and metaphorical music of the home as well as the skills needed for favourite pastimes. They adapt to the pressure and support of their parents and siblings, and so negotiate their distinctive choices of interest, subject and career.

These examples of interaction between individual personal growth and family values and culture may be interpreted through a variety of conceptual frameworks (e.g. class, culture, occupational habitus) but the very existence of such emotionally charged transmitters is fundamental to the understanding of education and social mobility. The inescapable problem is not that some children are helped or hindered by relative advantage or disadvantage but that home, family history and disposition are intrinsic, continuing dimensions of education. They condition every student's engagement with formal learning and contribute greatly to the diversity of response and achievement.

Some interviews (such as those with Julian, Lily, Charlotte and Tom) also highlighted the significance of attitudes towards risk. Parents can be cautious, advising, for example, against subjects that are perceived to be less 'academic' than others, or against careers that seem less secure or less desirable (e.g. acting/drama, special needs teaching). Some parents are influenced by insecurity in their own background to encourage their children into safe options in public service or towards other employment seen as reliable and stable.

Family interests and vocations

An important feature of the interviews was the frequency with which students reported interests, hobbies and activities derived from their families, including grandparents. Significant links emerged between interests that seem to have originated with other family members and respondents' later choices of subject and career pathway. Isaac, for example, accounted for his passion for animals in terms of his upbringing:

> When I was brought up my parents always had animals, we've always had pets, and I have mine that I look after myself; I really, really like the idea of a job with animals. At the moment I see it as just working at a pet store. In the future I would like to run my own pet store.

Isaac saw the future as winning a place at college to study for a diploma in animal management, and hoped to get a part-time job at a pet shop where he could gain experience. He 'would be gutted' if he could not have a job that involved animals. As he remarked: 'I've had cats, rabbits, hamsters, lizards; this has helped me to be good at caring for them.' Isaac's parents 'don't get involved too much' but they gave him advice and had bought home revision guides to help with mathematics, his weakest subject.

Gemma's love of animals had equally strong family origins, but her father had been very active in helping her develop her interest into a secure foundation for a professional career. She was one of Felix Holt's brightest A-level prospects and had received an offer to study veterinary medicine at a top university. She was brought up with animals, was passionately interested in them, and announced her goal of becoming a vet at a very early age. She said her motivation came from 'the type of person I am' but acknowledged her father's tendency to live his life through her. He was an intelligent computer expert who was uncomfortably aware that he did not try hard enough at school. He encouraged her to take every opportunity that came along and had arranged for her both work placements and a part-time job at an animal management company. This had proved so lucrative that she had been able to buy a car.

Ross (B group, South Park) told us that his father and grandfather had both played football to a high level and that he wanted a sports-based career himself. He was expected to achieve B/C grades at GCSE and planned to study a sports diploma course and A-level business at sixth form college. His father played for a second-tier club and his grandfather kept goal for a top professional team. Ross himself played for the school and county and aimed to progress into sports management and coaching. He said he was not interested in his father's property development company or his mother's pharmacy work, but could foresee the risk of ending up with no job despite having good qualifications.

Darren (B group, Felix Holt) is another respondent whose sporting connections had informed his leisure activities as well as his hopes for a future career. He told us he 'played for an under-8 team when I was 5' and that his uncle was a football coach who taught him the basics when he was young. Darren had already been offered a full-time job at a Premiership soccer club, conducting weekly outreach visits with schools and running after-school clubs to teach skills. His mother had contributed another dimension to his interests, arranging for him frequent appearances in films and advertisements since his babyhood. Darren aimed to study sports and exercise science at a post-1992 university and planned a career in personal training or with a soccer club.

A family aptitude for and interest in the expressive arts can also become a formative influence on young people's cultural development and subsequent careers. Louise's (B group, Felix Holt) father used to 'draw all the time' and she had always been interested in art. She was working on her portfolio to gain admission to a leading art school. Andrew (A group, Felix Holt) linked his own interest in wildlife photography to his mother's work as an illustrator. Drama and performance are at the centre of Charlotte's (Felix Holt, A group) life and she had been involved with local and community theatre for as long as she could remember. She had recently completed work experience with a theatre company. Charlotte was excited by 'the adrenalin rush of performing' but also enjoyed directing and the satisfaction of creating something special for an audience. When she was younger, she thought about acting or producing, but now she felt she would enjoy the role of drama teacher just as much.

Daniel (B group, Felix Holt) said he was seeking an internship with a music studio as an entry point for the wider music industry. He liked the idea of being creative and trying out different things, and emphasized the importance of music in his life as a source of relaxation and as an inspiration to try hard and achieve. The main influence came from his father, who had 'played the guitar since I was born or before'. Richard (A group, South Park) described himself as a 'music person' who was influenced by what was played at home, but was less certain about his future pathway. His father had a 'specific taste' and this continued to influence him. Richard enjoyed playing and belonged to a group of samba percussionists. Adam (A group, South Park) was a member of the youth drama club and relished drama and acting as a big part of his life, and told us that for him 'performing is fun'. But his academic interests were in science and maths and he envisaged a career related to this dimension of his life.

Some respondents bridled at following the example of parents and grandparents but were attracted to particular activities nevertheless. Owen's (A group, South Park) grandfather was an actuary and both his parents were scientists. He said he was reluctant to study science and maths because his parents work in that area but admitted he genuinely 'couldn't imagine doing anything else' and didn't think he would enjoy alternative subjects so much. Others found family examples inspiring. Rachael (A group, Felix Holt), for example, said that her extended family had been very important in developing her communication skills and desire to study foreign languages. She learned to be articulate from her mother, while holidays in Italy with her cousin inspired her to communicate with the rest of the family. She said 'you can do anything you want so long as you communicate'. Her mother wanted her to succeed at languages and helped organize a solo trip to Morocco, where she immersed herself in the culture.

These examples are consistent with other qualitative studies that document family interests and occupational genealogies. Our data confirms the finding that there can be a strong continuity of interests and vocational orientation within families and that individual choices belong to a wider pattern of adaptation to economic opportunity and change. Roderick Parker, for example, is an architect; his grandfather was a builder; his uncle was a building worker; and his niece married a builder (Thompson, 1997; Bertaux and Thompson, 1997). The stories detailed above are further evidence of the importance of family culture in transmitting interests, occupational comfort zones and a disposition towards particular activities and skills.

Habitus and dispositions

Students and families strive toward common goals, which transcend any mechanistic emphasis on results for their own sake. Schools and families combine to provide strong support to every child, and show equal ambition for and commitment to all students, even those least likely to succeed. Our sample gave few hints of the class-based resistance to teaching found at some city schools, with only two individuals at South Park self-consciously distancing themselves from the school regime. Interviews with the B groups at both schools yielded many examples of young people striving to do their best, quite often in the face of daunting family issues.

Even so, these unusually positive indicators cannot mask the troubling evidence that patterns of inequality continue to be 'imprinted from one generation to the next' (HMG, 2011), with family antecedents, circumstances and networks exerting a deep-seated influence on the ways that students in our sample view and interpret the world, and consequently on their educational and career outcomes. Although no student referred to social class and few reported themselves as disadvantaged or suffering from obstacles to future success, we found numerous instances of ill health, separation, divorce, unemployment and unskilled parental backgrounds impacting on identity, capability, aspiration and achievement.

Although both schools possess the effectiveness characteristics associated with high levels of achievement (Sammons *et al.*, 1995), a large minority of students at South Park (33 per cent) and at Felix Holt (40 per cent) fail to attain the much desired, mobility-friendly good GCSE threshold (5 A*–C grades including English and mathematics). The schools may well attract balanced or 'mixed' intakes, with fewer students than average eligible for FSM, but less-advantaged students continue to trail their peers, however dedicated their teachers and however determined they are themselves. Less-advantaged students continue to achieve less good results, even at highly effective schools (Cook, 2012).

As this account shows, the influence of family status, resources, models, values, culture and interests is by no means confined to the disadvantaged or the less successful. Almost all our students regard themselves as active participants in families that have transmitted economic, social and cultural capital, with long-term consequences for the children's dispositions and choices. Their stories are consistent with Bourdieu's claim that:

> habitus ... ensures the active presence of past experiences, which, deposited in each organism in the form of schemes of perception, thought and action, tend to guarantee the 'correctness' of practices and their constancy over time, more reliably than all formal rules and explicit norms.
>
> Bourdieu (1990: 54)

Our sample seems no less influenced by family and community antecedents, models and culture than previous generations, and there is some evidence that career tracks and choices also have deep roots in family history, although this requires fuller investigation (see chapter 6). There are indications that educational accreditation has become the currency through which social advantage is transmitted, rather than an instrument of transformation, and that the school system operates to differentiate students in terms of results and career tracks (Bourdieu and Passeron, 1977). For those who are young the future seems to be 'entirely in my own hands' but, below the surface, life and fate are subject to the 'past experiences ... deposited in each organism' (Bourdieu, 1990).

Chapter 5

Aspirations

Introduction

Coalition policy proposals construct social mobility in simplistic terms and encourage the view that young people should continually strive to climb the mobility ladder and pursue careers above and beyond those of their parents and extended family. As discussed in chapter 2, *Opening Doors* (HMG, 2011) sets out the government's commitment to ensuring that all young people have the maximum opportunities to realize their potential in the education and labour market. This commitment includes the provision of financial support for the foundation years, school years, transition years and adulthood, to ensure that people from all backgrounds can experience social mobility and fulfil their individual potential. The *Opening Doors* action plan assumes that everyone wishes to seek individual social mobility, and that inequality can be reduced by appropriate reforms. But policy-makers are less clear about what constitutes social mobility from one generation to the next, how mobility can be measured and how mobility might be made possible for all people. This is particularly significant since the number of top jobs compared with the size of the population is relatively limited, and many aspects of mobility are gendered. As we have seen in chapter 2, government conceptualizations of mobility are ubiquitous, problematic and highly individualized.

This chapter examines the respondents' answers to interview questions about their aspirations for the future in terms of their careers and family lives. These questions explored the students' primary concerns for the future, examining their aspirations, motivations and other sources of satisfaction and happiness. We examine five areas of aspiration and consider them in relation to the concepts of habitus and dispositions (Bourdieu, 1977a) and also to government views of social mobility.

The five areas of aspiration considered here are happiness, satisfaction, making a difference, status and wealth. These five themes were selected on the basis of the frequency with which they were cited in the interviews and their relevance to the research aims and objectives. The most frequently cited themes relate to happiness and personal satisfaction and to the pursuit of challenging activities that are exciting and rewarding for their own sakes. B group students in both schools placed an even stronger emphasis on family, happiness and 'getting along' than those in the A groups. B group students expressed a strong desire to please their parents and teachers, but also to be independent and have friends.

Aspirations

The five aspirations discussed in this chapter are defined below, indicating how we constructed and understood the themes that emerged from the interviews. These definitions are based on our respondents' thoughts about each area:

- Personal and professional happiness: the pursuit and accomplishment of individualized goals and aspirations. These goals related to future employment and aspects of private life, such as having children, in almost equal measure.
- Job satisfaction: having a future career that is challenging and stimulating, where every day is different and the work is demanding and testing.
- Making a difference: the desire to make a positive, measurable impact at work and in some instances the wider local community.
- Status: the drive to gain high-status employment that provides a degree of power and autonomy. It represents a desire for various forms of social mobility.
- Wealth: the accumulation of economic security and wealth and material advantage through a chosen employment pathway.

Personal and professional happiness

The most dominant theme across the two groups and the two schools related to the respondents' aspirations for personal happiness. This was cited as important by 17 of our sample. The theme of happiness related to respondents' future professional and personal lives; they were keen to obtain future employment and personal circumstances that, amongst other things, would make them happy.

Five students from the South Park A group said they sought happiness in their future work lives. Jason told us that 'in the future, it is having a job that I enjoy and that I reach through hard work, putting effort in and that has paid off in something I enjoy and I can get a good life from'. Noah echoed this sentiment, saying that 'as long as I've worked hard and feel I've been successful and enjoy the job, that's success ... not liking the job is what I fear and so pay is much less important than enjoyment of the job'. Isabella explained that for her, success in the future would be 'job satisfaction and happiness ... this is what marks successful people. You need enough money to pay for your house and family and a small surplus.' Isabella felt that focusing on either making money or achieving personal gain alone was not as important as seeking happiness. Ian also wanted to be happy with his future work and told us that there would be few benefits to being paid well if the job was dull, and that this would not feel like success to him. Sean too felt that enjoying a job and having job satisfaction would be an important factor for his future success.

All of these students are from economically privileged family backgrounds and their parents hold rewarding, professional employment. They all described happy family backgrounds where they were valued and supported economically, educationally and emotionally. Jason's parents have academic jobs at the local university, Noah's parents have professional private sector jobs, Isabella's parents are scientists, Sean's are professors and Irene's are musicians. Their dispositions towards paid employment emphasize the importance of securing both economic wealth and happiness in their professional and private lives. The similarities in their dispositions, which are influenced by a middle-class background, suggest a shared habitus that prioritizes high occupational status and seeks a more satisfying experience of work.

Six students from the South Park B group had similar aspirations to secure happiness as an important part of their future success. Jasmine and Anna desired happiness in their professional and private lives. This desire was again strongly influenced by their family milieu. Jasmine told us that her family life is quite advantaged:

> We have not been affected at all by the recession ... we are not financially badly off. I don't think my gender makes a difference as I'm one of three girls, and my mum was the one who has encouraged me and my sisters most of all [...] My mum says don't do it for the money, do it for the love of it. She believes if you enjoy it you should do it, not because it pays well. I think it is a good outlook for life, if you don't enjoy it, you shouldn't do it.

Anna's family had influenced her thinking too, particularly her sister who was undertaking a course that she really enjoyed. Anna felt that she would much rather 'do something I enjoy ... I'd sooner do something I enjoy rather than something I don't. It's what I'm happy with for my future.' In contrast to Jasmine, Anna comes from a large and economically disadvantaged family, and has experienced hardships and constraints as a result. Anna's aspirations for future happiness reflect a working-class habitus, where there may be a greater tendency to focus on happiness as an end in itself rather than on more middle-class, competitive, and high-status professional outcomes. But Jasmine's aspiration for happiness at work is inconsistent with such generalizations and confirms Bourdieu's (1977a) view of habitus as generative and structuring but also as disruptive and agentic, depending on the nuances of the family context.

The remaining four South Park B group respondents also aspired to gain happiness in their future employment. Gavin wanted to secure financial independence but also personal happiness, identifying this as an important marker of his future success. Freddie sought financial stability for his future children so that he could provide for them and treat them well. He wanted a life of happiness with them and so, while he would work hard pursuing his dream of opening his own restaurant, he would also prioritize family time. Nathan had a vision of achieving 'a perfect job, for example as a film director. I want to direct good films, make good money and have the perfect family life.' Finally, Isaac wanted to pursue a job in animal management that he acknowledged might not pay well, but would provide him with happiness. He told us that there is 'no point living a future you hate every day ... it's much better to have a job you like instead of moaning all the time about your work'. With the exception of Nathan, these students had parents in working-class, semi-skilled occupations, and their families had struggled financially. All four students reported happy home lives and wanted to reproduce this in their future. Their dispositions show 'an objective basis for regular modes of behaviour', which in this instance inclines them to seek to reproduce the family milieu (Bourdieu, 1990: 77).

The key difference between South Park's A group and B group students' aspirations for future personal and professional happiness relates to the social class backgrounds they reported. The desire for happiness in the future may reflect the students' desire to reproduce the family and professional milieus they experienced in their formative years. The social class of the family may be less significant than its stability and contentment.

Only two students in the Felix Holt A group told us that personal happiness was important for their future success. Andrew explained that for him:

> Success will be measured in terms of how I feel. So, if I get to the stage where I've made it as a photographer or conservationist, and I feel happy and content with what I'm doing, then for me, that's a measure of success ... to enjoy what you are doing at the present moment. How are you successful if you are not happy?

Andrew also had a supportive family background that he described as follows:

> My family has been a big influence, my mum especially. I've had a
> lot of influence from her. She's an illustrator doing a master's and
> she's been conscious to help me, take me to multiple trips to places.
> I couldn't have asked for more.

Rachael also valued career success and, whilst she had not yet worked out
the details of her plans, she was keen that her future should involve pursuing
a challenging career that uses foreign languages, because this would make
her happy: 'to me success is about being happy in what you are doing and
having a new challenge every day'. Rachael's family milieu was supportive
and nurturing:

> I come from a middle-class family, quite privileged in terms
> of things I get from my parents and I find no barriers, only
> opportunities, thanks to family members who help me get a foot
> in the world of work.

Rachael's habitus seems influenced by well-connected parents who value
education, enjoy professional careers and are generally happy and contented
in their personal and professional lives.

Four of the Felix Holt B group students thought of happiness as an
integral component of their future success. Holly explained that she wanted
to secure a job:

> in the zoo industry ... I'd like to be comfortable enough to live and
> perhaps to move out of my house so I'm not relying on my parents
> as much, maybe rent a house. To be successful in the future it is
> important to be happy and to be comfortable with where I'm at in
> my life, particularly in my relationships.

Tania also wanted employment that would make her happy and she wanted
to 'spend the rest of my life doing something I really love'. Lauren wanted
to gain a good degree and secure employment. She wanted work that would
make her happy: 'I don't necessarily need to be too comfortable but I want to
make enough so I can have the necessities of life, but the main thing is to be
happy'. Dean was keen to gain secure employment that provided a degree of
financial security, but happiness and enjoyment were more important to him
than getting to the top.

There are clearly some differences between the A and B groups within
each school and between the two schools in terms of family background,
values and culture in relation to the theme of happiness, but there are

similarities as well. The aspiration for future happiness raises some questions about the influence of social class on the individual and the aspiration to achieve social mobility. These respondents were interested in making enough money to live comfortably and have the necessities they needed for life, but this would be constructed as a success only if they were happy with their personal lives and future jobs. So, without happiness, the value of money and job security would diminish.

These accounts can be read in multiple ways and could be taken as a reflection of the naivety of youth, the value and importance of a secure and happy family life, or as evidence of latent individualism. Regardless of the plurality of possible meanings and interpretations, what is striking is their mismatch with the construction of social mobility articulated in *Opening Doors*, which pays no attention to the importance of happiness in young people's views of career success. There is no acknowledgement that being happy at work is important for overall well-being and that this happiness should have a role in social mobility policy. The government focus on unleashing potential and breaking down barriers to high-status, high-mobility careers is at variance with our respondents' talk about their future plans. The 17 respondents considered here were not expressing a desire to become socially mobile in their careers, but were more concerned with reproducing their current position. This is shown by their desire to earn enough money to ensure security, and to have interesting, stimulating and challenging forms of work, but, crucially, to experience a happy work and personal life.

The interview data suggests that the aspirations, desires and dreams articulated by our respondents in relation to personal happiness may be an obstacle to social mobility. These respondents are not seeking to move beyond their parents' occupations in terms of objective status. Subjectively they need to feel that there is an emotional value to the work they are planning to do in the future, not just an economic or status value. This point is further illustrated in the following discussion of the importance of job satisfaction.

Job satisfaction

For six respondents, achieving job satisfaction was mentioned as an important element of their desired success. This motive was more evident amongst the students at Felix Holt, with only Sean from the South Park A group telling us that 'having an interesting job is quite important' in terms of his future. Sean's parents are both professors and thus have high-status professional careers. He said that his parents had discussed the importance of job satisfaction with him and had attempted to impress upon him the value of a job that would provide satisfaction as well as financial security. Only one of the South Park B group students specifically identified job satisfaction as a future aspiration.

Only two students from the Felix Holt A group referred to a desire for job satisfaction. Adele explained that she wanted to secure a job where 'I know I'm going to learn something different, something new each day'. Adele felt she would find the process of learning something new every day deeply satisfying and that job satisfaction was an important dimension of success. Graham also wanted access to a job that would provide satisfaction and told us that 'salary is really not too important for me; I'm going into a programming-based job, could go into loads of areas, e.g. game design, software development, robotics – I'd be interested in all of those'. He was keen to ensure that his future would be spent in a job that was interesting and stimulating rather than one that would simply provide wealth, status or upward mobility.

Three students from the Felix Holt B group talked about the importance of job satisfaction. Nick was excited by the idea of a job that would require him to live on the edge: 'I want to be doing something not in an office, but meeting interesting characters, I want new experiences all the time, not 9 to 5 every day ... that would provide me with job satisfaction which is important to me'. Claudia had similar aspirations for a job that would enable her to be:

> doing something satisfying and it needs to be out of the ordinary ... Not the same routine each day but something spontaneous. This would make me feel I was fulfilling my potential and making sure I achieve my potential each day.

Molly told us that she was not making plans for five years' time but hopes to be in an enjoyable job:

> I'm a lifeguard in the sports centre and I like it but I don't want to be doing that for the rest of my life ... I can't see me doing that in my thirties. I want a mature and satisfying job that's interesting.

All of the Felix Holt students who talked about the importance of job satisfaction had parents with reasonably high-status occupations, including as an accountant, engineer and underwriter. Thus, the respondents' habitus and dispositions are framed by their parents' professional lives, and this framing is reflected in their own desires for the future (Bourdieu, 1993b). For example, Claudia's father was a policeman who enjoyed his job and got a lot of satisfaction from serving his local community. He was a significant role model for Claudia and his experiences had inspired her to seek job satisfaction, suggesting that her dispositions were prompting choices for the future that led towards social reproduction. Nick's father was an engineer working in a highly professional environment that he found demanding and satisfying. Like Claudia, Nick's habitus and dispositions were influenced by his father's positive experiences of work and the subjective value he attached to his employment.

Our respondents' desire for occupations that will provide them with opportunities for job satisfaction is, again, entirely absent from policy-makers' expectations. These latter pay little attention to the importance of working in a challenging and stimulating environment. Policy assumes instead that upward mobility involves achieving financial mobility, status and the accompanying access to power (HMG, 2011). This theme again highlights the mismatch between the government's view of mobility and those raised by some of our respondents.

Making a difference

Three students from South Park A group, one in the Felix Holt A group and one member of the Felix Holt B group said they aspired to future employment that would enable them to make a positive difference and have a positive impact on their environment. Making a difference was an aspiration with a noticeably gendered dynamic. Four of the five respondents who hoped to make a difference in order to feel successful in the future were females. They resembled the 'good girls' in studies that explore the operation and impact of femininity on school-age girls who are selfless, caring and nurturing and who seek to bring happiness to those around them as a way of realizing their own happiness (Francis, 2000; Skelton and Francis, 2009).

Three members of the South Park A group wanted to make a difference. Zoey told us that her future success could be realized only if she had made a difference in some sort of way, and that this would bring her happiness: 'as long as I've made a contribution to the world, even if it's tiny, I'll feel I've been successful'. Emma sought to make a difference for herself, but also to make her family feel proud of her. She said that:

> If I can make my family proud I will really feel I've achieved something. I want to make a difference. For example, I was in a show and it was nice for my family to come and say how proud they were of me, it made a difference to them.

Ellie explained that for her, future success was also about making people feel happy, which would in turn make her feel happy. She wanted to 'get to the place where you want to be, feeling you mean something to other people, the world'. She was keen to pursue a career that could enable her to make a positive difference to people's lives.

In the Felix Holt A group, only Rob said he wanted to pursue a future career that would make a difference. He was somewhat philosophical in his discussion about this and said that:

> Einstein said you should measure true success by the value you give back to wider society. For me that carries significant value. So you don't see many millionaire or impossibly rich scientists and that fits with me and my desire to be a scientist. Since I was very young, I've always been more interested in influencing the future of humanity rather than getting rich myself; I shan't complain if I get rich but it isn't my primary goal.

Rob was altruistic in his hopes and plans for the future and was highly committed to pursuing a future in science. His parents were in professional occupations with his father working in IT and his mother as a teacher. Their influence on him was clearly a factor shaping his aspirations for the future; they wanted him to find work that would enable him to make a difference.

Holly was the only member of the Felix Holt B group who mentioned that she wanted to make a difference, in her case by working 'in the zoo industry ... doing something in relation to conservation is important to me, building up and breeding rare species and then introducing them into the wild'.

These examples illustrate the complexity of the habitus and dispositions within our sample and show that the combination of family values and individual aspirations provides space for agency and difference, despite the potential impact of structural inequalities. Whilst making a difference is a gendered and feminized aspiration held predominantly by girls who want to give back to the community, its presence among the aspirations of the students does also point to a more community-aware and collaborative view of success. This in turn confirms that not all young people have the same goals and desires for the future, and that not all young people are as individually focused and selfish as they are often represented.

Status

However, there are several students in our sample who defined their future happiness in relation to maintaining, obtaining and securing future status and power. Only students at South Park (in both the A and B groups) referred to a concern with gaining status. All those aspiring to secure future employment status were male.

Alaster told us that he was 'excited by the opportunity of getting into medicine, and the status it will confer ... It's a very different profession from those pursued by my family who are very old-fashioned and normal; my Dad's a salesman.' Alaster was a significant respondent in our sample as he was one of the small number of students who said he wanted to obtain higher occupational status than his family. He aspired to achieve objective, linear and rational social mobility of the type envisaged in government policy documents.

Elijah was also keen to gain a high-profile and high-status job. He was interested in pursuing a 'technical job, like economics, or even international relations ... I want to do something that has a high profile and I want to study difficult subjects. For me success will eventually mean being a professional in one of these careers.' Elijah's parents, unlike Alaster's, both had high-status professional careers. Bourdieu argues that habitus emerges through primary socialization, that is:

> [a] practical evaluation of the likelihood of the success of a given action in a given situation which brings into play a whole body of wisdom, sayings, commonplaces, ethical precepts (that's not for the likes of us).
>
> (Bourdieu, 1977a: 487).

Elijah's habitus and dispositions were influenced by high-status academic achievements that were an important dimension of his family milieu and had shaped his desire to achieve a similar, even elevated, status in his own future. He identified a professional career as something appropriate and attainable for him.

Julian, from the South Park B group, also wanted a job with status. His preference, like Elijah's, was influenced by his family background. He told us that 'from a young age I've wanted to be a policeman ... My granddad was a policeman, which influenced me a lot, and I really like the idea of working up the ranks to a higher-status position.' Julian was from an advantaged background and it was not surprising, therefore, that although he was happy to enter the police force in a relatively junior position, he said he wants to climb the career ladder and gain a senior position. His comments indicate that he possesses valued forms of social and cultural capital, including access to networks, cultural resources and experiences and appropriate family values to assist him in his pursuit of status. He voiced a high level of confidence and assurance in himself and in his future success.

These respondents' desire for status may not represent a conscious wish for social mobility but is nevertheless consistent with Gove's wish to produce a more meritocratic society. Their commitment to gaining status and power in their careers indicates an ambition to achieve an individual outcome and advantage for individual benefit.

Wealth

The fifth theme discussed in this chapter relates to the respondents' aspirations to achieve economic wealth. Three of the Felix Holt B group and one of the A group were keen on finding careers that would deliver material wealth. They were motivated to ensure their future financial security partly because they had all experienced financial hardship at home. Tania wanted to 'move up and get the money, I like the money associated with veterinary'. Similarly Dave felt that for his future success 'earning more money is very important to me'. Simon was keen to:

> make a comfortable amount of money, not sure about going to the very top, not the way I work, but I wouldn't complain if I did, but I like hands-on work, where I communicate with people. I can be a good team leader, depending on the tasks, and it would be a nice route to get there (to the top).

Darren had his sights on a successful football career and was aware of the financial rewards attached to that:

> Next year I'm hoping to play for the first team; [at a previous club] I got paid £10 per week; in the reserves I don't get paid, but in the first team I get an average of £250 and the captain gets £750. There's better chances and you have to believe in yourself.

Kylie, an A group respondent, told us that 'I don't know what I want to do as a job, but I know I want to be well off ... that would be a success'. They were not necessarily aware of the job they wanted to do, but they were keen to secure high earnings.

Darren and Tania told us it was important to them to move upwards and secure greater financial rewards than their parents. They reflected the sentiment that hard work and desire will be enough to secure the financial rewards they are seeking. Like those respondents who sought upward mobility and status, they fully believe that success and failure rest entirely with the individual. Their responses do not acknowledge the sorts of bonding and bridging social capital exploited by the middle classes, who have access to particular networks and resources and who gain, for example, high-status internships, privileged academic pathways and employment prospects (Putnam, 1995). This leads the respondents to emphasize their individual agency above all other elements of becoming successful. Their status as agentic, choosing subjects form the root of their belief in the meritocratic possibilities provided by their state education, family backgrounds and belief in themselves.

Only one respondent from the South Park B group openly discussed his desire to make as much money as he could, and acknowledged that he was strongly motivated by the desire to accumulate wealth in the future. Ross told us that:

> I would have to place myself as lower than my Dad, who got a degree in quantity surveying, and he now shares a company with three other people ... he used to have his own quantity surveying company. I would like my Dad's money ... I suppose I'd like to do better than my parents and definitely want to earn more money and get the qualifications I need to be able to carry on ... There are no obstacles holding me back.

Like Alaster, Ross was keen to move beyond his parents' economic position and so gain a form of social mobility. Despite his view that there are no obstacles in his path, the likelihood of him achieving the wealth he desired was uncertain: Ross was predicted C grades in his forthcoming examinations. Yet despite this potential constraint, he presented himself as highly ambitious and displayed a keen sense of individualism regarding his future success. He was single-minded and focused on achieving his goals of making money and attaining the kind of financial independence that his father had managed to secure.

Ross's desire to obtain a level of wealth and employment mobility that would take him beyond his parents' present occupational status is in keeping with the government's conception of social mobility. Ross articulated individualized goals for his future that centre on economic and professional mobility and are in line with Gove's aspirations for young people. Ross may be constrained in the early stages of his career if his actual examination grades are as predicted, but his motives may well carry him forward all the same. He seemed untroubled by such thoughts.

Aspirations

Five areas of aspiration influence our respondents' constructions and understandings of what will constitute future success. Respondents identified other aspirations, but these tended to relate to gaining the qualifications necessary for preferred post-compulsory educational pathways. The subjective motives selected for discussion here illustrate the extent to which the majority of respondents expressed desires for the future at variance with the assumptions made by policy-makers. However, there were also some examples of goals and aims that resonate with government policy, including the desire for status and the desire for material wealth. Whilst these were mentioned by a very small number of respondents, their inclusion exemplifies the range of responses we encountered.

This chapter has shown that, whilst status and wealth are important to some of the respondents, a critical mass disavows these as goals for years to come and very few respondents expressed a hint of dissatisfaction with their family background or lifestyle. Some were inclined to equate the notion of 'success' with choice and the freedom to pursue personal goals and interests but, as argued in chapters 3 and 4, the idea of rising beyond parents and family in terms of professional position, status and/or wealth was almost entirely absent from the interviews, and very few respondents expressed a desire to 'climb ladders' and rise up beyond their parents. Where there was evidence of this desire it reflected a wish to ensure their future financial security, a motive often stemming from experiences of financial hardship. Our sample's vocational access and aspirations seem to be woven into their family environment, and in general to match their academic ability. The students' reflections provide, therefore, a large number of examples of the transmission of cultural capital and evidence of social reproduction.

For most respondents the important thing is to have sufficient money to do interesting things and to take part in enriching activities. Very able respondents (i.e. A group students) were particularly strong in expressing a desire to be part of an inclusive community, rather than to live in a privileged 'bubble'. Their competitiveness seems to relate to GCSE examinations and sport, rather than to the social world beyond the school.

Female and male students were equally likely to stress personal happiness, family priorities and contentment with intrinsically rewarding careers. Female and male students also stressed happiness and intrinsic work fulfilment rather than a desire to acquire wealth for its own sake, and often described themselves as interested in money only in so far as it enables choices. However, it is noticeable that the majority of students who want to make a difference to other people's lives are female, while those seeking status are male, indicating some gendered differences (Skelton and Francis, 2009).

This chapter has shown that by far the most common and significant aspiration amongst our respondents is the achievement of personal and professional happiness. Discussion of the first three aspirations shows the limitations of government ideas about mobility that emphasize employment status and the pursuit of wealth and neglect the important role of happiness, fulfilment and making a positive difference.

Chapter 6

Choosing the future

Introduction

We have seen that our students have many school experiences and attitudes that are consistent with policy-making assumptions about social mobility. At both schools most students described themselves as hardworking, competitive individuals eager to progress to the best possible grades and successful working careers. They perceived the future as being in their own hands and dismissed the idea that there are constraints on what can be achieved. They saw their 'landscapes of choice' as individualized and unfettered by underlying structures (Ball *et al.*, 2000).

Ethnicity, gender and class were barely mentioned, except to dismiss the possibility that they could be sources of hindrance. Only two students (at South Park) commented on unequal opportunity within the school system. The government has no need to 'challenge low aspirations and expectations' at Felix Holt or South Park because the students have internalized almost completely the idea of their own individual responsibility and believe that qualifications are an important route to career success. Respondents emphasized the extent to which they were encouraged and challenged to succeed by their teachers, who were often cited as role models. The schools organize Key Stage 4 (KS4) work experience for all students; Felix Holt also provides similar opportunities in Key Stage 5 (KS5). There is abundant evidence that teachers intervene to ensure appropriate placements for individuals, regardless of ability or relative advantage/disadvantage. An assistant head at Felix Holt, with oversight of the sixth form, was emphatic about the work done to encourage students to aim for the best universities:

> We know the amount of work and effort needed to get into Russell
> Group universities; it is about giving kids the right advice. Too
> much says go to university, while there can be too little on the type
> of university. I have a concern that people come into teaching for
> different reasons – some have a pastoral view that is important
> for the disadvantaged but sometimes what is lacking is academic
> rigour; to say you can aim higher. I came into teaching because I
> wanted people to go to Oxford.

There is a shared perception across both schools that all students, of whatever ability and background, can achieve their full potential and progress towards appropriate and worthwhile careers. The inclusive congeniality and good reputations of South Park and Felix Holt seem to have led respondents to believe in their own unrestrained agency and opportunities – the world is their oyster – and to confirm the individualist hypothesis that suitably reformed schools may transcend the unequal structures that feature in so much of the literature on youth and careers (Furlong and Biggart, 1999; Ball *et al.*, 2000).

However, this evidence in support of individualized, rational models of student choice, academic success and career progression is balanced by other indicators that provide less support for the notion that equal opportunities necessarily contribute to increased social mobility. We have seen how family culture and interests precondition respondents' developing identities and self-image, help shape the pathways they find attractive and influence their subject choices. Almost all students said they were content with the lifestyle and culture embodied in their homes and parents. Occasional reservations were expressed about one or other parent, but no respondent said they were at odds with their home and the values and goals espoused by close relatives. Respondents described future success in terms of personal and family happiness, job satisfaction, making a difference, and having an adequate income to support modest family needs. Many students explicitly rejected the idea of striving for wealth and upward mobility. Although participants reported themselves as individual agents with few impediments to desired goals, they also described themselves as active, positive members of valued families and their local communities.

This chapter aims to review the extent to which social mobility policy expectations are justified by the evidence gathered in this study about our students' choices of academic and career pathways. Do high-performing schools like South Park and Felix Holt provide a secure foundation for hardworking, upwardly mobile young people, enabling them to transcend disadvantage, humble origins and/or dysfunctional family circumstances? Can an extra £2.5 billion investment through the Pupil Premium 'radically improve their educational outcomes' (HMG, 2011: 6)? Or does it remain true that 'deep-seated inequalities in the British labour market' steer young people towards divergent career paths and trajectories based on their levels of accreditation (Hodkinson *et al.*, 1996: 7)?

We analysed the 88 interview transcripts for evidence that:

- Students have clear, rational understandings of available options, routes and pathways through secondary and higher education, training and the workplace.
- Students' 'horizons for action' have broadened to include progressive pathways and trajectories, associated with aspirational 'careership' routes not taken by other family members nor in past generations (Hodkinson *et al.*, 1996).
- Choices and outcomes transcend disadvantage and other unequal structures, with family patterns and influences less significant for our sample's career and life planning than for the urban cohort investigated by Ball *et al.* (2000).

This chapter draws on additional data from the Felix Holt Family Employment History (Appendix 2). The 42 sixth form students at Felix Holt each filled in a simple form to indicate his or her own current vocational aspiration and the remembered occupations of their grandparents and parents. Although incomplete and at times fragmentary, Appendix 2 provides valuable contextual information that improves our understanding of how families influence individual career choices and contribute to social fluidity.

Our data is discussed below in the context of five main themes that emerge from our interviews: (1) school structures that individualize, sort and label; (2) family patterns and influences on occupational preferences; (3) students' realism and risk management as they negotiate academic and work careers; (4) obstacles to assessing and achieving upward mobility; and (5) fluidity and stability through school and family.

School structures

Our respondents belong to a generation that entered the school system in New Labour's high summer. They have been more extensively tested and examined than any previous cohort of English school students, and have been subject to an intensive hyper-accountability regime supposed to increase efficiency and performance (Mansell, 2007). School and external assessments have provided detailed, continuous feedback on their achievements (or lack thereof) from an early age, and have conditioned expectations through repeated assessment cycles. At South Park and Felix Holt, students are given predicted grades and targets in every subject and their progress is monitored closely, with appropriate interventions to remedy slippage as and when required.

South Park

Lily and Ian reflected on the pressure generated by continual assessment, monitoring and feedback, and illustrated the extent to which their lives have been dominated by marks, grades and their future significance:

> Ian: We have minimum target grades you are supposed to achieve on your worst day but you are expected to do better. It is hard when the minimum target grades are A*. In some subjects I'm not getting there but teachers seem to think A* is my minimum and chase me up and ask why I'm not.

> Lily: In some subjects I'm above target, in some subjects on it, and in others I'm not achieving it. It's not due to lack of effort.

> Ian: The minimum is set in stone too early, so they don't know how well you can do.

> Lily: It's based on your year 6 SATs[1]. Because of earlier good marks you can struggle to reach the target and marks can drop drastically.

> Ian: In English I was really pleased with my A-grade reading and listening marks, but the teacher called me in and said it wasn't good enough.

Despite an occasional sense of injustice about a particular mark or teacher comment, the GCSE candidates at South Park accepted the feedback they were given and worked hard to match the high expectations designed into the process. Elijah, for example, said:

> To know that I've done well, to get good feedback, it gives that confidence you are on the right track for what you are seeking. When you get to sixth form, you've got to know the difference between going in the right or wrong direction.

Adam's attitude was typical of the A group at South Park. Determined to succeed, he accepted full responsibility for his examination results and adopted long-term plans to improve:

> It's all about taking little steps towards my big goals, like getting GCSEs, for example, controlled assessments in Spanish help you to be sure you can do the small things towards the best overall grade. In the future I'll have to think about adapting my work ethic so I can get into the best university I can; I need to be more focused –

I'm not sure how big a gap there is between GCSE and A level and must prepare for a worst case scenario.

Respondents were in the process of applying for sixth form colleges, so their comments often reflected their awareness of the implications of their subject choices, both for university entrance and for future careers. Although their course selections arose mainly from intrinsic interest and personal enjoyment, they were also keen not to close doors. Faith, for example, said she had a strong interest in the performing arts but was careful to pick 'subjects that show I am academic'. Lily was pretty confident that she wanted to work in a special school, especially after an enjoyable work experience, but nevertheless chose psychology amongst her A levels to 'keep your options broad'.

B group students were no less persuaded by the validity of their predicted grades and targets, and no less keen to work hard to improve. Samantha said she hoped 'to exceed my minimum target grades. I'm down for Cs but hope to get the Bs to get me into sixth form college.' Anna was headed for a vocational course in childcare but saw success as hitting targets and achieving required grades. Alice told us that 'I can't focus in exams, I struggle, I'm a person who learns by doing rather than listening' but was determined to secure the D and C grades needed for entry to the FE college course for the uniformed services. Isaac was headed towards another vocational course but told us firmly that 'I'm very determined to push myself to the highest limits to get what I want and deserve'. Julian praised South Park because when he joined 'I was expected to get just passes but I've improved because the teachers have pushed me and kept me working hard, because they knew I had potential'.

Students at South Park were acutely conscious, therefore, of their assessment data and acknowledged the impact of predicted and actual GCSE grades on their embryonic plans. Without exception, A group students oriented themselves towards the more selective of the two sixth form colleges, while B group members were aligned with the less-selective option or the local FE college, with most hoping for admission to vocational courses. Almost all South Park students described post-16 goals that were strongly influenced by realism about their qualification prospects, and most also had well-developed occupational preferences. Test and examination results, student grouping strategies and binary curriculum structures seem to play their part in creating distinctive academic and vocational tracks, evident in Table 6.1.

Table 6.1: Student tracks at South Park

Cohort	Number of students	Typical estimated GCSE results
High academic track	24	A* grades
Academic track	3	B grades
Creative academic or creative vocational track	2	C grades
Vocational track	17	B–E grades
Total	46	

All 24 A group members at South Park, expected to achieve straight A* grades at GCSE, were strongly committed to the 'high academic track', with Oxbridge and Russell Group universities in their sights. Their self-confidence and expectations for the future were notably high, reflecting a long history of success in tests and examinations from primary school onwards. Rose, for example, intimated that 'success for me at school is getting 11A* grades in the summer and that's in line with my predicted grades ... Success for me would be getting into Cambridge University and going on to have an outstanding academic career.' Hannah was equally confident, commenting that she'd 'like to pursue a career in medicine; my aspirations are to get good grades, go to a top sixth form college then get to a good university, there is no ceiling on my dream of becoming a doctor'. Zoey's goal was also straightforward: she plans to follow a first degree with PhD research into high-energy physics or marine biology. Isabella wanted 'high grades to go to prestigious universities'. She said:

> I'm thinking about doing a degree that opens more doors into higher-rated jobs. You always want the best you can possibly get, you use on-line rankings to check out universities, find the places you want to go.

Alaster presented as exceptionally confident and ambitious. He hoped to be a doctor because 'that's the ultimate goal, no-one in my family is medical – I want to do something worthwhile and change the world, creating something or finding something out that will save and change lives'.

By contrast, B group members were already adapting to scaled-down, less-prestigious ambitions (in the cases of those estimated to attain B/C grades) or less-favoured colleges and/or vocational goals (in the case of those estimated to attain D/E grades). Julian said he had wanted to be a policeman from an early age; Carl hoped to be accepted on a level 2 football coaching course; Patrick wanted to be a plumber; Jordan said he struggles at school but hopes to be accepted at the FE college to follow a level 3 sports and leisure award. Freddie needed at least a B grade to embark on a professional cookery diploma at the FE college. Cathy expected to achieve mainly C grades but hoped to study for an art diploma at the less selective sixth form college. Anna has struggled with 'loads of writing' and already had an interview scheduled for a place on a childcare course at the FE college. Sandy couldn't wait to leave school and planned to combine an apprenticeship with a hairdressing course at FE college. The year 11 pastoral leader said these career choices were due to the disproportionate number of students in the lower percentiles 'who haven't seen working life modelled'. He felt that 'lower down the scale, more and more there is a complete lack of aspiration'.

All this is consistent with the conclusion that basic decisions about education and work are firm and quite stable by the early teenage years, although many students adjust their expectations downwards with growing knowledge of likely GCSE results and awareness of entry requirements for particular options (Rojewski and Kim, 2003). After 15,000 hours[2] of hyper-accountability teaching and testing, it is less than surprising that young people have a clear and early understanding of their position in the academic and occupational 'pecking order' (Furlong and Biggart, 1999). Group A students consolidate their positions on a flexible and relatively open-ended 'high academic' track, with a small number holding the possibility of a slightly less prestigious university in reserve. Continuous examination success enables A group students to delay work decisions and to hone preferences between well-paid professional possibilities, but relatively less successful B group members with middle (B/C) and lower (D/E) grades find that options narrow rapidly as they acquire less-transferable, less-regarded skills. They are steered towards vocational courses, many of them gendered on traditional lines, especially for girls (e.g. childcare, hairdressing, art). This illustrates the extent to which gender intersects with social class to limit the possibilities for some students (Brah and Phoenix, 2004).

Felix Holt

Selective admission arrangements and a significant age difference reduce the validity of direct comparisons between the pathways chosen by students at the two schools, especially those followed by the B group sample. Respondents at Felix Holt are on average two years older than those at South Park and were selected for the sixth form on the basis of their GCSE results. For admission to post-16 courses, students have to achieve five passes at grades

A*–C, including English or Mathematics. The normal entry requirement for an A level or vocational course, as set out in the school's Admissions Policy for the Sixth Form, is a B or a merit in that subject at GCSE/level 2. As a result the Felix Holt B group is less representative of the school's year 7 entry than the B group at South Park. Over thirty students are recruited each year from other schools, adding to the size and viability of the post-16 enrolment but also contributing an unknown but probably favourable addition to the relative quality of the student body. Felix Holt students in both groups were completing rather than choosing their sixth-form courses, and had substantially greater experience of advanced study, work placements and part-time employment. They were also more mature and so better able to offer insight into their journeys through school and college towards higher education or the workplace.

Table 6.2: Student tracks at Felix Holt

Cohort	Number of students	Typical estimated A level results
High academic track	12	11 students estimated A grades 1 student estimated B grades
Academic track	14	6 students estimated A 4 students estimated B 4 students estimated C
Creative academic Or Creative vocational track	5	Mainly estimated C grades
Vocational track	11	Mainly estimated C–D grades
Total	42	

Despite these limitations, Table 6.2 shows a marked contrast between A group and B group destinations resembling that observed at South Park (see Table 6.1, p. 110). All but one of the A group members had a laser-like focus on Oxbridge or Russell Group universities while B group students spanned the spectrum from less-prestigious universities to direct employment. With additional A-level and vocational qualifications behind them, Felix Holt students had stronger expectations of the job market than the 16-year-old school leavers at South Park, but the difference between 'high academic', 'academic' and 'vocational' tracks is nevertheless striking and significant.

The 'academic' track, relatively under-populated at South Park, was more important at Felix Holt, where 14 students were doubtful about their grades and eager to choose less challenging universities.

Predicted and actual examination results[3] emerged as a strong influence on academic and career decisions, with students generally more concerned with university offers and their own prior track record than with internal monitoring and targets. Respondents on the 'high academic' track were clear about their goals. Rachael, for example, said that she would like to go to Durham University: 'I need AAB; I'd prefer to get higher than that, because it is important to me to work hard to show I've achieved at A level.' Graham was content with AAB to secure a place at Birmingham while Jack seemed happy with an A*AA offer to study chemistry at Oxford, believing that it 'should be relatively easy because all I need is B in the last chemistry module'. Gemma needed A*AA to read veterinary science at Cambridge and seemed relatively untroubled by the challenge.

'Academic' track students, including six group A members expected to achieve good grades, were less confident about their chances of making the grade. Lucy had not expected her offer from the University of East Anglia to be so high (AAB) while Marilyn said her estimated grades (ABC) were lower than her offer from Winchester (ABB). Mary was so concerned about her prospects that she gave up going out and limited her work at Tesco to make more time for revision. She needed A/B grades to study physiotherapy at Bournemouth or Coventry. Tania was frustrated that her estimated grades (ABD) were below what was required for veterinary medicine and was working on various strategies, including retaking below-par subjects or switching to a more accessible degree course. Other students, like Darren, were repeating courses and hoped to squeeze into universities via the clearing system, in his case to study sports science in preparation for becoming a personal trainer.

Some B group students, like Matt, were following vocation-related courses that led to university. He hoped to study business with market relations at a post-1992 university and to progress to an internship, possibly with Coca-Cola or Cadbury. Others, like Nick, were simply eager to leave school and 'start earning rather than living off my parents'. He didn't want to go to university or stay in education and had thoughts of starting a business linked to technology-based industry, where his A levels in electronics, computing, physics and business should be useful. Tony felt that getting out to work would be the better option for him, especially when university fees are going up. Dave also hoped for a job straight from school, in his case with the police. He told us he has never 'fancied' university and chose the sixth form because his friends were there and because the police recruitment age meant that he had a year to fill.

Vocational-track students pursued a variety of employment opportunities, sometimes related to their part-time jobs, as they adapted to the possibility that their grades (C/D) would not help them to secure places in higher education, or concluded that further study would be unproductive for them (see Table 6.3).

Students have a personal history, attitudes and interests that influence their decisions, but expected examination results seem to be a critical factor in prompting 'ideal' and often ambitious choices, and also in persuading some to limit their hopes to a small number of acceptable alternatives (Gottfredson, 2002). Those with minimal risk of academic failure (A group) overwhelmingly aim for prestigious universities and occupations, while those who perceive themselves to be at risk of not achieving required grades (many members of the B group, but also less-confident A group students) have lower occupational aspirations (Patton and Creed, 2007).

Table 6.3: Vocational track intentions at Felix Holt

Student	Employment intention	Expected grade	Track
Harry	Tesco (chain supermarket)	BTEC	Vocational
Dave	Police	C	Vocational
Tony	Accountant	C	Vocational
Simon	Media producer	C	Vocational
Nick	Self-employment	C/D	Vocational
Layla	Trader	C/D	Vocational
Mary	Physiotherapy	A/B	Vocational+[4]
Holly	Zookeeper	C	Vocational+
Dean	Advertising/marketing	C	Vocational+
Joyce	Groom, equine studies	C	Vocational+
Darren	Personal trainer	C/D	Vocational+

The 'higher academic' (A group), 'academic' (mainly upper B group) and 'vocational' (mainly B group) tracks identified at South Park (16+) and Felix Holt (18+) illustrate the ways in which internal school processes, including assessment, curriculum structures, feedback and guidance, contribute powerfully to students' perceptions of their identity and self-efficacy, and condition their aspirations and choices. These students have been individualized, developed, labelled and sorted, with well-defined accreditation tracks shaping and channelling their ambition and future opportunities. An

RE teacher at Felix Holt suggested that students tend to accept where they have been positioned on the strength of KS2 test scores, with the result that 'the kids in the lower sets aren't really aware they can achieve high'. She claimed that testing and tracking limit young people's aspirations.

Family employment patterns and influences

Social mobility policy would be right to emphasize the role of education in opening doors for all, regardless of background, provided these internal school processes operate fairly and rationally, so that individual agents could develop their abilities to the full and choose appropriate career goals, unconstrained by other, less-visible variables and influences. The scope for improved upward mobility mainly depends on the extent to which high quality academies, like South Park and Felix Holt, produce self-sufficient, equal opportunity environments, where everyone with a modicum of ability can work hard and make rational, progressive decisions, unhindered by 'the circumstances of their birth; the home they're born into ... or the jobs their parents do' (Nick Clegg in HMG, 2011: 3, quoted above).

As related in chapter 3, our respondents believe strongly in their own agency and responsibility, and regard the apparent limitations of income and personal circumstances as challenges to overcome rather than as constraints on future opportunity. This is consistent with two ESRC studies of South London students born between 1979 and 1980. Respondents viewed their decision-making in terms of individual choice, rather than as the result of structured constraints. Young people blamed themselves for their lack of success and seemed to embrace a culture of individualism prompted by, and interrelated with, social changes that foster increased reflexivity and individualization (Ball *et al.*, 2000). Old-fashioned class differences were less visible in a youth landscape where the London informants produced narratives for a 'contingently reflexive life-time biographical project' that deals with new risks and opportunities (Giddens, 1991, quoted in Ball *et al.*, 2000: 2).

Our cohorts, born in 1993/4 (18-year-olds at Felix Holt) and 1995/6 (16-year-olds at South Park), were equally inclined to accept responsibility for their own futures and to embark on reflexive biographies. Young people described themselves as individual agents, responsible for their school results, career paths and even life courses, and seemed to accept the individualizing, sorting and labelling processes of school as entirely fair and natural, with available opportunities related directly to ability and effort. Our respondents' narratives contain, nevertheless, stories and insights that reach beyond individualism and suggest the extent to which students know the importance and influence of their families, including the parts played by previous generations.

South Park

Every one of the group A students at South Park embarked on the 'high academic' track named a range of academic, scientific and technical interests and aspirations that were closely related to their parents' backgrounds. Rose, for example, whose researcher father held a chemistry PhD, aimed to study natural sciences at Cambridge before progressing to a PhD herself: 'I want to do something to do with academia; knowledge and learning is what I've always loved. Especially in scientific research.' Zoey, whose parents were both scientists, identified marine biology or high-energy physics as potential areas of doctoral study. Sean, whose parents were both professors, wanted to work in science, though he didn't have a particular course in mind: 'I'd like to study at a high level, in a lot of detail'.

Elijah (father a professor, mother a leading researcher) was considering economics, international relations or aeronautical engineering as career paths, but emphasized his desire for a high-level technical, professional job, with the potential to 'spin off into high-tech manufacturing'. Isabella (both parents scientists) hoped for a career in sports medicine. Owen (grandfather an actuary, both parents scientists) aspired to study science and mathematics. Chloe (academic parents) was keen to study medicine and said that her friends and family had helped her understanding of medicine and medical careers. Some of her friends' parents were doctors or surgeons and 'from what they've said it sounds really interesting'.

Family connections and influences were equally important for B group members, especially in accessing local opportunities. Sandy already worked Saturdays at her mother's hairdressing salon and described plans for improving the business when she qualified. Patrick was expecting C grades but liked doing hands-on work and had no desire to sit in an office. His parents wanted him to be a plumber and regarded it as a 'good trade'. He saw plumbing as an attractive career option. Gavin was keen to follow his father into the police force. He was completing a diploma in public services (for bus drivers, librarians, police officers etc.) and said his father was trying to find him a suitable training opportunity for when he left school. Jordan's father used to play football and would 'kick a ball around with me, he'd show me how to improve'. Jordan himself had won a scholarship to an FE college and intended to take a level 3 sport and leisure course, with a view to becoming a professional footballer. Isaac grew up in a household with animals and wanted to study animal management before working in a pet shop, an ambition supported without question by his father (a decorator) and mother (a cleaner).

A mathematics teacher reported a sense amongst his departmental colleagues that some students were content to reach the minimum level at Key Stage 3 (KS3) and lacked 'the desire to push on', despite the school's 'purposeful attempt to raise aspiration'. He spoke of an 'unofficial view' that there is a split between children from academic backgrounds and others 'who live in the village who are not going to perform as well'. People from the immediate locality seemed content with their lives and were generally less ambitious. The maths teacher worried that children from such backgrounds would lack role models and so have little idea how to progress beyond familiar environments.

This did not apply to Nathan, whose career horizons seemed very different from other B group members, with their willing acceptance of less-prestigious vocational options. His ambition to become a film director seemed unrealistic in view of his predicted C/D grades but he was encouraged nevertheless by his advantaged family. He planned to take the media national certificate and study film studies at the less-selective sixth form college, to be followed by the London Film School or the New York Film Academy:

> I think my parents will fund it, they want me to get the best of life; some of my friends think film director is too big; I say I know what I'm doing and can do it. Ever since I was little my dad's been showing me films, creative ideas, *Lord of the Rings*, so I thought I'd like to express my ideas on the big screen, used to write stories and cartoons.

Nathan was determined not to settle for the limited options pursued by many less academically successful students. His outlook contrasts sharply with others of apparently similar ability and suggests that, although young people exercise agency, their aspirations are inflected by the social contexts in which they live and by their sense of what is normal for people 'like me' (Archer *et al.*, 2010). The concept of economic, cultural and social capital, transmitted through the family and community, helps make sense of the dissimilarity between the A and B groups at South Park, especially in their attitudes towards available academic and career paths (Bourdieu, 1986).

Felix Holt

As we turn our attention to the 18-year-olds at Felix Holt and examine the roles of the students' families in shaping vocational aspirations and decisions, we can supplement our interview data with an additional, longitudinal source of information, the family employment history details supplied by each respondent (Appendix 2). Despite the limitations of the data, this source increases our knowledge of family patterns and influences, enabling us to consider our sample's goals in the context of jobs chosen by their parents and grandparents.

The Family Employment History (Appendix 2) details three generations, including grandparents born mainly in the 1940s and 1950s, parents born mainly in the 1960s and 1970s, and the respondents themselves, born c. 1993/94. Overall, the table captures a great variety and complexity of experience, with families and individuals drawing on diverse resources and subject to fluctuating fortunes, often related to the local and national economy. Families have adapted in different ways to the economic and educational opportunities that have unfolded through the last fifty years. Upward trajectories can be found, though progress is rarely simple or linear, with many apparently successful individuals subsequently losing ground through divorce, illness, recession and unemployment. Two significant trends are evident from close scrutiny of the Family Employment History and the students' interviews:

- Over time, family members often work in similar or analogous occupations.
- Parents are a strong influence on occupational choice and status aspiration.

RELATED OCCUPATIONS

Over 60 per cent of students reported two or more relatives in similar or related jobs. Lance's father and grandfather were telecommunication engineers, for example; both Jack's parents were accountants, while three of his grandparents were involved in motor transport. Lucy's mother and paternal grandfather were both telephone company managers. Rachael's father and three of her grandparents were involved in carpentry or gardening. Rebecca's family included three teachers. Andrew, Colin, Gemma, Kylie, Lance, Michael and Nick all had multiple family members involved in engineering, electronics and electrical work. Charlotte's father and grandfather were trade managers, while her mother was one of three teaching assistants in the cohort whose children planned to become teachers. Mary's grandmothers both worked in private business while her father ran his own computer repair company, and her mother was an accountant for her husband.

PARENTAL INFLUENCE

Over 30 per cent of respondents reported a strong vocational link between their parents, other family members, and their own academic and career preferences at this stage. Paul's mother was a teaching assistant; Paul wished to teach. Tony had extensive work experience with his father's accountancy firm and was committed to a career in accountancy. Dave was keen to follow his father into the police force. Harry had decided to join Tesco, a chain supermarket, where his mother worked.

The interviews confirm that many students develop a vocational disposition related closely to family interests, hobbies and occupations (see also chapter 4). Several A group members referred to close relatives as the inspiration for their career preferences. Lance, for example, spent a lot of time at his grandfather's house when he was young, and remembered that 'he was always doing electronic stuff and that has led to where I am now'. His parents had encouraged his interest, and had made sure that he participated in relevant extracurricular activities, trips and work experience. At the time of his interview, Lance had decided to become a chartered engineer and recognized that his grandfather (an electrician with British Telecom) and parents had helped develop the groundwork for his career.

Michael also reported that he had picked up a lot of knowledge and understanding from family members involved in engineering. Rebecca, whose grandmother was a nurse, felt that her mother had been overbearing in her 'desperation for me to become a doctor' but she nevertheless valued her family's encouragement to pursue a medical career, and their practical help with work experience. These manoeuvres illustrate the sophisticated ways in which family resources may be deployed to maintain status and class advantage, with successful parents offering informal guidance and access that smooths the path towards highly-regarded universities and occupations (Ball *et al.,* 2000).

Less academic students (grade C or lower) were also aware of the need to mobilize available family resources to secure a toehold in the job market. Tony had already worked for his father and was prepared to sacrifice his independence for the time being. Dave was also realistic and recognized that it would be difficult to follow his father into the police: 'You can work as hard as you like but if they are not recruiting, they are not recruiting'. He was rather sorry that his father's contacts and service no longer guarantee entry. Dave said he was reconciled to becoming a special constable and joining the waiting list.

A business studies teacher said that many students were reluctant to look beyond the local area and were inhibited by a lack of self-belief and self-esteem. She reported that when she wore her 'careers teacher hat' and asked about the future or their aspirations, 'they don't think they should dream big, and that's what holds them back from going beyond parents and what they could achieve themselves'. She said that some students chose to stay on in the sixth form 'not because it is the best place but because they don't want to venture out, don't want to try something else'. She wished she could inject them with 'the swagger, the confidence' of the privately educated students she encountered through extracurricular activities. She said that boys from one school in particular 'know where they are going; it's built into their world from day one, they know the university, the course and what they are going to do'. An economics teacher agreed that students somehow embodied their family background: 'The older they get, the more you can distinguish those from a money background, especially from an affluent area, from the way they hold themselves, the clothes they wear, the way they speak'.

One of the pastoral leaders, a teacher of business studies and economics, disagreed that students were held back by lack of confidence, claiming that 'the students who come my way in year 11 and year 13 are very ambitious'. Simon is an example of a B group student who expected to rise in the world despite weaker predicted grades. He outlined how he would enter the media and work his way up through family contacts. One relative owned a media production company and had contacts at the BBC; his father's partner was a TV director who had worked with celebrities on cooking shows. His family experience indicated to him that you don't necessarily need a degree and can climb your way up from lowly positions. He said he 'can get a job through contacts' because people liked his positive attitude and found him a likeable lad.

Simon, like Nathan at South Park, had been strongly influenced by his successful family to 'dream big' and to look beyond the usual pathways open to someone with his predicted grades. Despite relatively poorer academic results, both boys possessed an element of the 'swagger, the confidence' observed in private schoolboys by the Felix Holt careers teacher. The contrast between these two and other B group students confirms that socio-economic status is a significant influence on occupational goals, and that young people's aspirations are shaped by their identities, embodied practices and structural locations (Rojewski and Kim, 2003; Archer *et al.*, 2010).

Young people at both schools explained how their identities, values, aspirations, dispositions and interests had drawn, and continue to draw, upon varied sources of capital (see chapter 4). Regardless of background and ability, every student's account was permeated by an awareness that the family, past and present, continued to be significant in their lives. This is consistent with Ball *et al.'s* (2000) finding that families were more significant in their respondents' social and educational experiences than expected, with parents in particular playing an important role in career and life planning. A markedly similar pattern emerges from Vincent's (1997) study of 444 respondents interviewed between 1969 and 1973. Parents, older siblings or nearby kin were instrumental in arranging three out of every four posts obtained by this twentieth-century cohort. It seems that families are not as easily overcome as individualism suggests.

Realism and risk

This evidence confirms that family background and educational tracking have an interrelated, reciprocal influence on respondents' thoughts about the future, and work to condition respondents' views of available opportunities. Respondents 'horizons for action' are constrained, therefore, by a realistic assessment of what is available and by their evolving ideas of what is suitable for applicants like themselves. As a result, social variables (class, ethnicity, gender) have a continued structuring effect that leads to unequal life chances, apparently similar to those experienced in the 1990s by members of a study cohort on a government training scheme (Hodkinson *et al.*, 1996). This does not mean that the students' agency in their own lives should be discounted or that impersonal forces predetermine their careers. On the contrary, respondents provided numerous examples of intelligent planning and action.

South Park

This was true at South Park, although students were primarily concerned with choosing a sixth form college course to match their interests and ability. Respondents explained the options they were considering and expressed clear vocational ideas, but these were seldom specific; they indicated a direction of travel rather than a particular job or role. As we have seen, Elijah spoke of 'career options' in economics, international relations and aeronautical engineering and was aware that you could become an engineer, 'then spin off into a high-tech manufacturing company'. Rose was already committed to the idea of a PhD and scientific research, but her vocational dreams included space travel and Arctic exploration.

Group A students in general seemed convergent in their pursuit of the 'high academic' track. They were inclined to connect a favourite school subject (science, history) with an obvious occupation (e.g. researcher, teacher). Respondents seemed driven by their enjoyment of particular subjects and by the influence of one or more family members and teachers. Owen, for example, said mathematics and science were for him: 'I do try in those subjects because I enjoy them, and that's why I've done well. I want to go to degree level, and in terms of jobs and careers, see myself doing science/maths.'

Sophie too was certain about her favourite subject and envisaged a future career based on it:

> I'd quite like to go into teaching because I'm passionate about history and would like to share. I read lots of history and watch lots of programmes, and try to further my knowledge. I just generally find it interesting, the past is a fascinating place, not that it may help me in the future, and I just love it.

Although most A group students had clear preferences, they were aware that their vocational plans were at an early stage and expected that their GCSE results and sixth form courses would provide the additional information they needed to find a route through higher education towards a professional career. Isabella, for example, said nothing was 'set in stone' and that she needed more time to 'see how I do in A levels' and 'find what I really like'. She was 'thinking about doing a degree that opens more doors into higher-rated jobs'.

B group students, who were expecting less good GCSE results, were often less certain about the possibilities ahead, or expressed doubts about goals the A group were inclined to take for granted. Leah, for example, was planning to study sociology, English literature, photography and mathematics at the less-selective sixth form college, but was 'not sure what I want to do after that. I've chosen a range where I could get into any job.' With her family background (sick brother, non-working parents) she also had serious reservations about university on financial grounds, pointing out that the fees 'may pre-empt resources you want for something else'. Max was considering working abroad, doing charitable work or 'building something' and was applying for an eclectic range of sixth form subjects, including psychology, philosophy, film studies, art and design. These subjects were 'all things I love doing, they're all creative'.

Alison was coping with the competing demands of school, part-time work, and social life, and with her parents' recent divorce. Despite the upsetting family break-up, she was anxious to 'get on with it' and get the grade B needed for admission to her chosen course in sport and psychology. Uncertain about her prospects, she was realistic but proactive in juggling the different aspects of her life:

> I'm predicted a D in Spanish, on average Bs and Cs, and an A in Physics ... I've already had part-time jobs, I'd hope to continue

with work on the side of my education, I haven't got settled plans ... having a job limits your social life. I have work Friday, Saturday and Sunday nights. I'll do my homework when I get home ... I'm getting time off work towards my exams, they're very understanding of my school life.

Young people, especially those expected to achieve average and below-average grades, have to juggle complex demands on their time and energy, and often make pragmatic decisions about part-time jobs, social life and homework on the basis of little information. Although these decisions may have long-term consequences, the outcomes are far from inevitable.

Felix Holt

Students at Felix Holt, two years further on with their school careers, displayed a more developed understanding of relevant education and employment opportunities, and often entered into sophisticated calculations about the future. Tom and Charlotte (A group students), for example, showed strategic awareness and realism in developing their plans, but the main obstacle for both of them seemed to be a simplistic tracking system that did not match their needs. Tom was unsure what he wanted to do and was reluctant to follow the logic of the academic route on which he appeared to be progressing well. Although he was good at English, he was not convinced that he would derive much enjoyment from a full degree course. He said he found it 'hard to commit to things' and feared that if he jumped into university he would come to regret it within a couple of years. He argued that universities no longer guaranteed a job and that he might have a 'head start' if he entered employment 'three years sooner than other people'. Tom's reservations (like Leah's at South Park) illustrate the ways in which some young people now worry about the value of higher education and seriously consider the advantages of alternative courses of action.

Charlotte was also frustrated by the implications of the tracking system. She was anxious to reconcile her proven ability (A grades were predicted) with her passionate interest in theatre and drama. She had been involved in shows from a young age and thought that it 'would be brilliant to act' but had become aware that drama was deemed a vocational and possibly less prestigious subject. She had gained the impression that 'drama is not a subject to go with if you want to succeed in life', remarking that:

I wasn't offered A-level drama, only BTEC. I wish I'd been offered A-level so I could study Shakespeare, look at scripts more, look at things in depth. BTEC is not worthless but I feel that if I'd had the chance to do A-level it would have helped me with options. Some universities don't like BTEC.

Charlotte was determined to be a drama teacher, nevertheless, and planned to do work experience with a theatre company before going to drama school.

Some students were busy making their own luck by building on work experience and part-time jobs. Dean was recommended to Sky Media by a teacher at Felix Holt who had once worked for the company; Dean enjoyed a week's placement that was 'spot on for my interests in telesales and advertising'. Gemma's work placements, including a part-time job with an animal lecturing company, gave her valuable experience that refined her vocational interest, so that she was thinking of wild animal medicine rather than her original plan to care for companion animals. Tony's plans had developed through 'doing stuff for my Dad at Canary Wharf' and with other companies 'my Dad's got me into'.

Poised before major public examinations, however, many borderline students were concerned about the risks they faced. Passionate about dreamed careers, they were close to the point when they might have to adjust their sights downwards or even change direction entirely. Tania, aware that she was a good talker and would do better with oral exams, had begun to face the reality of below-par predicted grades. She talked about re-sits and biology-based alternatives if she did not achieve the results demanded by veterinary college. Marilyn's predicted grades were also lower than required for her first choice place. She felt that her examination skills 'aren't up to standard; I struggle with essay writing' but still hoped that in the end she would do better than expected and so gain admission to a post-1992 law school.

Layla had decided against university because her predicted grades were 'pulling me down, so I'd rather not go there'. She had chosen instead to pursue a career as a trader, much influenced by an economics teacher who had worked on the stock market. Joyce was determined to work with horses 'at all costs' but had discovered she hated further mathematics and chemistry. She had given up hope of veterinary medicine and talked about equine studies, a subject geared toward people working with horses rather than in the laboratory. The cold reality of the results to come was impinging on these students and obliging them to contemplate reduced 'horizons for action'.

The strategies and plans that these accounts show our respondents developing should not be interpreted as the inevitable outcomes of underlying structures and processes. The students always emphasized a strong sense of personal responsibility for their decisions and goals. They saw themselves as active agents, negotiating individual pathways through the transition from school to work, and into the early years of employment. Social interactions (with parents, education/training providers and the workplace) were closely interrelated with their pragmatic decisions. As they mused on academic and career possibilities, most students were aware that apparently small decisions could have long-term consequences, and acknowledged that with time their aspirations and career trajectories might be subject to change.

A good many young people had witnessed threatening changes in family circumstances and could envisage having to cope with similar life-changing events. Even when their choices appeared predictable and straightforward, respondents saw themselves as pragmatic agents, searching for the best pathway and the most suitable opportunity. Young people's perceptions of future courses and careers may be deeply rooted in their identities, life histories and individual experience, but our data suggests their decisions, like those in Hodkinson *et al.*'s study (1996), are neither determined nor unfettered, are subject to constant revision and adjustment, and have the potential to produce uncertain, unpredictable trajectories and outcomes.

Upward mobility

The Felix Holt Family Employment History (Appendix 2) provides an unusual glimpse of 42 young people as they launch themselves into the world, and suggests the extent to which they have the potential to climb above their parents. Almost all have identified pathways suitable for their aptitudes, interests and expected results. Some, especially in the B group, cling to aspirations that may later be revised downwards in the light of actual results. But it is too soon to judge their ultimate occupational success or to assess their qualities as striving members of professional, commercial and voluntary organizations. These students have well-defined goals, however, that indicate the nature and status of their likely early employment. Does this information support the government's assertion that educational qualifications are the key to mobility?

Table 6.4 details the occupational backgrounds and aspirations of the most academically successful students at Felix Holt, all expected to achieve straight A grades in their final examinations. These are exceptional students with great potential. Colin, for example, aims to be an electronic engineer. Adele intends to become a lawyer, Gemma hopes to be a veterinary surgeon, and Graham has his sights on becoming a software developer. None of these careers guarantees top earnings and some named destinations have the potential to be much better paid than others, but the intended routes all have scope for progression. Much depends on an individual finding and exploiting opportunities in the future. As Martin suggested, life can be like

125

mah-jong[5] 'where you can go along without success, then suddenly a couple of opportunities and you win the game'.

Table 6.4: Felix Holt high achievers: occupational background and intentions

Student	Father's occupation	Mother's occupation	Career intention
Adele	Accountant	Carer	Lawyer
Andrew	Carpenter	Illustrator/artist	Wildlife photographer
Ben	Car sales/driver	Nurse	Teacher
Charlotte	Trade manager	Teaching assistant	Drama teacher
Colin	Clothes company	Confectionery industry	Electronic engineer
Gemma	Computer engineer	Support worker	Veterinary surgeon
Graham	Insurance management	School admissions	Software developer
Jack	Accountant	Accountant	Chemist/researcher
Kylie	Drainage engineer	Communications manager	Teacher
Lance	Telecommunications	Teaching assistant	Electronic engineer
Lucy	Printer/unemployed	BT manager	English degree
Martin	Chef/restaurateur	Hairdresser	English degree
Michael	Wholesale delivery	Shop work	Electrical engineer
Paul	TV sports producer	Teaching assistant	Teacher
Rachael	Carpenter	Investment banker	Work abroad/ languages
Rebecca	Managing director	Teacher	Cancer research
Rob	IT/redundant	Teacher	Research chemist
Tom	Manual work	Customer service	Undecided

There are significant difficulties, however, with using this data to assess prospective social mobility. The lack of detailed information and the reliance on self-reported, non-standardized job descriptors (e.g. 'wholesale delivery') provide an unreliable, invalid foundation for measuring the potential earnings disparity between the fathers listed and their offspring, male or female. Our qualitative interviews cannot illuminate or resolve the statistical controversies that arise from recent attempts to arrive at firm conclusions about male social mobility through the rigorous analysis and counter-analysis of birth cohort data (Blanden *et al.*, 2005a; Gorard, 2008).

The Family Employment History, however incomplete and anecdotal, suggests nevertheless the inadequacy of a conception of improvement and mobility that is limited to tracking individual males. Respondents' interviews and job histories exemplify at a local level the extent and significance of marked changes in female occupational status over the last fifty years. The 'high academic' pathways selected by the group A girls at South Park also illustrate the rapid growth of female participation in education and higher-level employment in recent years. This remarkable change in the sources of family position and prosperity prompts a new and contrasting understanding of intra- and intergenerational mobility. It demands a very different investigative approach, one concerned more with households and family networks than with isolated pairs of fathers and sons. Women can no longer be excluded from calculations of individual and family mobility: the Family Employment History helps us understand why this is so.

The occupations listed for grandmothers, mothers and their daughters are consistent with national trends. They reflect both the increasing numbers of women participating in education since the 1960s and a parallel improvement in female access to well-regarded academic and career pathways. There were 118,000 students at university in 1962/3 (Robbins Report, 1963) and 1,367,330 reading for first degrees in 2011, with women occupying over half of the latter undergraduate places (Broecke and Hamed, 2008; HESA, 2011).

Few grandmothers of the 1940s/50s generation seem to have acquired academic qualifications or to have followed well-defined careers in the modern sense (Appendix 2) (Dyhouse, 1995). The majority of occupations recorded are routine clerical or manual jobs, with the occasional nurse or teacher standing out as exceptional in a world of female employment comprised of cleaners, gardeners, shop assistants, factory workers, carers, hairdressers, receptionists and office staff (Deem, 1981).

By contrast, women in the next generation (our respondents' mothers) seem to have benefited from improved access to sixth forms and further and higher education, and to have progressed into more demanding roles. The survey documents two accountants, two managers in telecommunications, an investment banker, a banker, an engineer, and a number of non-routine administrators (e.g. a payroll manager and an admissions secretary). Nurses and teachers have become more numerous than in the previous generation, while there are few references to factory and manual work, and none to gardening and agriculture. Schools have become significant employers of women, with 26 per cent of the mothers employed as teachers, teaching assistants and education-sector office workers. No student listed his or her mother as a housewife. Sometimes the mothers have better jobs than their husbands. Andrew, Ben, Lucy, Rachael, Rob and Tom all have mothers with greater occupational status than their husbands. Women may also become the main breadwinner following redundancy, ill health, separation and divorce (Appendix 2).

A comparison between the mothers' stated occupations and their daughters' intentions suggests there is considerable potential for a further advance in the qualifications and work roles of women. Table 6.5 shows the maternal side (grandmother, mother, daughter) of 13 Felix Holt families, selected because the female respondents seem to have the greatest chances of social mobility. These daughters are poised to outperform their mothers and grandmothers in terms of professional status and income. They have seized opportunities less readily available in the previous generation, and are aiming for employment as teachers, lawyers, veterinary surgeons, cancer researchers and journalists, rather than following their mothers as teaching assistants and office workers. This is much less the case for the 'high academic' track daughters at South Park, where successful young women appear to be emulating their highly educated mothers. There is a marked, unusual concentration of female professionals amongst South Park parents, possibly associated with the nearby university and science park.

Table 6.5: Felix Holt: women's careers

Student	Grandmother's occupation	Mother's occupation	Career intention	*Father's occupation*
Adele	Caterer/cleaner	Carer	Lawyer	*Accountant*
Charlotte	Cleaner	Teaching assistant	Drama teacher	*Trade manager*
Gemma	Not known	Support worker	Veterinary surgeon	*Computer engineer*
Rebecca	Nurse	Teacher	Cancer research	*Managing director*
Claudia	Self-employed	Admin worker	Primary teacher	*Police officer*
Lauren	Not known	Payroll manager	Chemist	*Police officer*
Layla	Housewife	Teacher	Trader	*Business transport*

Louise	Shop assistant	Teaching assistant	Artist	*Not known – 'drew a lot'*
Marilyn	Teacher	School office	Lawyer	*Managing director*
Mia	Not known	Exam invigilator	Journalist/ historian	*Software developer*
Paula	Cashier	Teaching assistant	Teacher	*Carpenter*
Tania	Not known	Doctor's receptionist	Veterinary surgeon	*Boat builder*
Zara	Not known	Clergy	Lawyer/ own business	*Builder*

The young women featured in Table 6.5 confirm the proposition that success, however defined, derives from the long-term accumulation of advantages that enables fortunate individuals to benefit from changes in social and economic circumstances (Gladwell, 2008). Although some of the mothers shown occupy relatively modest positions in the labour market, the fathers are generally successful, skilled individuals, often with private business interests or professional qualifications. Adele's desire to be a lawyer may signify a potential leap forward from her mother's work as a carer, but is less remarkable in the context of her father's profession as an accountant. A similar possible jump for Tania, from her mother's duties as a doctor's receptionist to her own hopes of becoming a veterinary surgeon, seems more predictable when her father's boat-building business and her previous private education are taken into account. These daughters come from skilled, advantaged families, so they are well positioned to exploit the expansion of higher education and changes in the nature of available employment.

This undoubted generational progress in the status and quality of work available for women changes our perspective on social mobility and upsets traditional assumptions about the male-centred nature of female status and mobility (Acker, 1973). We can no longer concentrate on individual male earnings, because women's income and position is equally important. Partnerships, successful and less successful, sustained and less sustained, have become a vital influence on life chances and trajectories, and have long-term significance for family members, both adults and children. Women's and men's social and economic prospects are today closely associated with the nature and quality of the relationships formed by their mothers and fathers, and also with the prosperity of their own partnerships (Coats, 1994).

This is confirmed by the A group respondents shown in Table 6.4 (p. 126). These high-achieving students, male and female, with the partial exceptions of Lucy and Rob, come from prosperous double-income households, with one or both parents occupying senior, well-rewarded positions or running their own businesses. The 24 A group students at South Park, whose expected examination results are equally promising, are in a similar position. For bright students at both schools, there is considerable potential for above-average earnings and social mobility.

This potential need not translate into upward mobility, however, especially in the economic climate following the banking crisis of 2007–2008. Greater competition between well-qualified candidates for a reduced number of high-quality jobs, increased tuition fees, and daunting house prices are amongst many reasons why young people from successful double-income families may struggle to do better than parents blessed by relatively benign economic conditions in the past. Participation in sixth form and higher education has grown so that advantaged students now have to secure admission to prestigious universities simply to maintain their family's position, never mind to advance further.

Fluidity and stability

Our data shows the myriad ways in which good schools and families help students succeed and so contribute to social fluidity, with capable young people acquiring qualifications that were not available for many in the previous generation, and so adapting to changes in the structure of the labour market. The large number of students progressing through South Park to the highly selective local sixth form college, and growing Russell Group participation at Felix Holt, prove that excellent comprehensives can compete at the highest level, with their best students moving on to distinguished careers and some winning Oxbridge places. Our respondents exercised considerable agency in negotiating academic and career transitions, and their trajectories varied greatly as a result, with individuals seeking opportunities and making the most of their advantages, howsoever defined and accumulated (Gladwell, 2008). Students understood the pathways through GCSE and beyond, although their choices were shaped by their underlying dispositions and by a pragmatic assessment of whether an option is suitable.

As we have seen, however, there are marked differences between the A and B groups at both schools that relate to the students' social and cultural capital, curriculum tracking and their examination results. Members of the B group, with a few notable exceptions, have poorer examination prospects and have adjusted their 'horizons of action' downwards to expect relatively low status and income. Social class seems to operate through depressed academic attainment that feeds back into students' self-perceptions and lowers their aspirations (Furlong and Biggart, 1999). Our data provides a poignant example of this process, with Rose looking forward to a Cambridge PhD followed by space travel or Arctic exploration, and Isaac declaring himself content with the prospect of working in a pet shop.

Even in these two outstanding schools, examinations and tracking seem to measure, reward and pigeonhole particular types of ability, rather than to facilitate strategies that encourage everyone to succeed. Social context, inherited attitudes and assumptions, curriculum tracking and examination results tend to discourage 'unrealistic' aspirations and eventually guide most B group students towards lower-status vocational destinations. The family, rather than the individual, seems to be the key unit in the process of stratification and acts to perpetuate and crystallize inequality. Family patterns and influences were demonstrably significant for our students' life and career planning, while educational provision seems to have reinforced rather than transformed the processes of social reproduction, so contributing to social stability (Archer *et al.*, 2010).

Notes

[1] Standardised Assessment Tasks (SATs).
[2] Rutter *et al.* (1979) estimate 15,000 hours as the time children spend at school.
[3] At the point of interview, many students had module results to hand.
[4] Vocational+ hopes to achieve C grades for entry to a vocational course in higher education, sometimes at the second attempt.
[5] A Chinese game for four people, played with tiles.

Chapter 7

Conclusion – dream or reality?

Introduction

We have reviewed the UK government's aims and objectives in developing social mobility policy for England and have closely analysed 88 young people's thoughts and feelings about their family backgrounds, aspirations, education and future careers. We chose our respondents from two academies with 'good' and 'outstanding' characteristics, similar to those that policy-makers wish to see adopted across the country to increase performance and mobility for everyone (HMG, 2011; DfE, 2010a). South Park and Felix Holt both emphasize high-quality teaching, hard work and aiming high. They have high expectations and set demanding targets. They are prototypes of the new academy regime, expected to emulate top independent schools despite accepting the full ability range and receiving per-pupil funding that is approximately 70 per cent less than at the average private school (Gunter, 2011).

We have formulated five statements (see chapter 1) to define the conditions we expect to find at high-performing schools where expectations and standards are being raised in ways that should eventually produce greater social mobility. We need to be sure the government's aims and objectives are coherent and realistic, and to discover the extent to which these two new academies have succeeded in producing students who strive to advance beyond their parents in terms of academic achievement, status and income. Close analysis of government policy documents (chapter 2) and our interviews (chapters 3–6) provide evidence for the following summary review of these statements.

Policy framework

1. Policy-makers articulate a rigorous conceptual framework for competitive individualism and social mobility (chapter 2).

Since the early 1990s, politicians have demanded that education should bring about an achievement-based, meritocratic society that rewards hard work and ability rather than birth and background. Michael Gove is but one of those urging that the social order should become fairer, through greater equality of opportunity, and more efficient, by ensuring that determined individuals can rise through the ranks to occupy senior positions in industry and commerce. But the concept of a 'meritocracy' where people progress according to their intelligence and effort has been problematic since it was invented. *The Rise of the Meritocracy* lampooned the notion that 'no spending was more productive than spending on the generation of brain-power' and mocked the continuous assessment of intelligence 'throughout school life' (Young, 1961: 75, 77).

Tony Blair admired the book, but seemingly without understanding the satire, and in office he made spending on increased brainpower his top priority (Miller, 2013). Sceptics question whether meritocracy is desirable and suggest that a person's merit or social usefulness may not be guaranteed by her or his ability to pass examinations and gain admission to prestigious colleges (Hayes, 2012). Some mobility researchers even doubt whether relative mobility can be improved, while other voices claim that Britain is already a meritocratic society (e.g. Goldthorpe, 1987; Saunders, 2010).

This may help to explain why policy-makers have aimed to improve opportunity, especially for the disadvantaged, but have been vague about the nature of the mobility they hope to encourage and the type of society they would like to produce. The Coalition has multiple aims that are not necessarily consistent with one another, and is inclined to express them in very general terms. The government is resolved:

- to improve relative mobility chances for able and hard-working individuals;
- to increase the proportion of lower-class candidates who gain admission to Russell Group universities;
- to raise everyone's status and skills;
- to forge a society that is more equal and less divided at school and work.

It is often unclear how these large goals will be achieved, except through broad improvements in school quality and opportunity.

Gove (2012, unpaged), for example, has condemned our 'profoundly unequal society' in strong moral terms, but the Coalition's 'indicator set' is designed to monitor individual and institutional performance, rather than to check whether society is becoming more or less unequal. The Gini coefficient is not included among the large number of planned mobility indicators, but state school performance is to be compared with that of the highest-attaining independent schools, and measures of social background are to be developed so that post-graduate employment destinations can be monitored for signs of improved mobility. Schools and universities will have to collect data about student destinations as an indication of employment mobility (HMG, 2011: 77).

The Coalition's emphasis on 'common sense' individualism enables policy-makers to avoid the danger inherent in defining their goals too precisely and also to avoid the problems involved in bringing about social change. Ministers do not speculate about causes and consequences but instead belabour schools for their failure to close supposed performance gaps. They concentrate on an individualist narrative where education must inevitably open new opportunities for young people, regardless of their background. Their story is straightforward and widely believed but nevertheless provides an incomplete account of the intricate social processes that have unfolded over generations.

The Coalition policy framework does not sufficiently recognize the role of families in shaping young people and their perceptions of the world around them. Gove asserts that schools are the most important variable in children's intellectual development and that personal circumstances need not impact on students' learning ability, interests, outlook and behaviour. Since top independent schools produce highly successful people, he believes there is a moral imperative to ensure that *every* child has access to an academic education of similar quality, with well-trained teachers and a rigorous curriculum (Gove, 2012). The role of selection, family wealth and habitus in producing differences in school performance is not considered.

This concentration on individualist solutions has seriously limited the conceptual resources available to the government. Mr Gove has embarked on major reforms to increase social fluidity, for example, without investigating the extent to which Britain is already a meritocratic society and without considering the non-educational variables that may contribute to current rates of relative and absolute mobility. The Coalition has not acknowledged the 40 per cent increase in inequality between 1974 and 2000, and does not ask whether economic changes between the two dates may be more relevant to social mobility trends than variations in the quality of schooling (Institute of Fiscal Studies, cited in Barker, 2010b: 24).

Opening Doors (HMG, 2011) accumulates the statistics of disadvantage, but does not ask why different social groups have such contrasting experiences or draw on the work of authors who place such data in a wider context. Nobel Prize winner and former chief economist at the World Bank Joseph Stiglitz (2012), for example, argues that the rampant greed of the wealthiest one per cent has brought about unprecedented inequality and the collapse of opportunity for ordinary Americans. The dream of prosperity for all has evaporated. Strong links between increased inequality and poor outcomes have been observed in both Britain and the US, with epidemiological studies confirming that health, education and social problems are worse in less-equal societies (Wilkinson and Pickett, 2009). The government does not recognize that social mobility is unlikely to increase in conditions of acute inequality, however much schools improve, and does not acknowledge that large-scale youth unemployment is a serious threat to equal opportunities in the workplace.

The Coalition also discounts the influence of social class on education, but in so doing ignores important ways of understanding structural inequalities and their influence on schooling. Although social class identities have grown weaker and the workplace is no longer dominated by muscular trade unionism, class is 'everywhere and nowhere, denied yet continually enacted' (Savage, 2000; Reay, 2006: 290). Class categories continue to make sense to large numbers of people and can be used to show predictable differences in life chances and choices across a spectrum of employment groups (Goldthorpe and Mills, 2008).

But policy-makers still underestimate the links between poverty and examination performance. Webber and Butler (2005) demonstrate that neighbourhood type is the single most reliable predictor of GCSE performance. Two former directors of the University of London Institute of Education agree that there is a strong negative correlation between most measures of social disadvantage and school achievement (Mortimore and Whitty, 2000: 10). Figure 2.1 (chapter 2, p. 33) shows that gradations in GCSE point scores track gradations in neighbourhood wealth. Social structure clearly exerts an important influence on student outcomes.

By comparison, schools seem to have limited impact on relative outcomes. Figure 2.3 (chapter 2, p. 47) suggests that high-performing schools are no more likely to 'close the gap' than low-performing ones, and that poverty is remarkably resistant to school-level interventions. This conclusion is consistent with studies that have reported school effects to be small. Gray *et al.* (1995), for example, found that once allowance was made for social background and prior attainment, the degree of between-school variance remaining to be explained could be slight. The individualist view does not allow for the possibility that most of the differences between schools can be attributed to their social mix, with concentrations of advantaged or disadvantaged students producing contrasting performance profiles (Thrupp, 1999). Gove is indignant that England has 'one of the most stratified and segregated school systems in the world' but his reforms do not include measures to tackle structures that produce unfair results (DfE, 2010b: 1).

Unfairness is endemic, even in a system that is supposed to redress the consequences of unfairness, as Martin Bright has discovered:

> We found a merciless pecking order that worked in favour of children already favoured by their birth. In Birmingham we saw a secondary system brutally segregated along class lines. The pecking order mirrors the national pattern: highly elitist private schools, selective grammar schools performing well above the national average, girls' and church comprehensives with adequate results, then the rest.

(Bright, 2005:1)

Inequality, social class and relative advantage are therefore essential concepts for understanding why communities and families are so varied in their experience, outlook and dispositions, and why children are set on positive or negative educational and vocational trajectories from an early age. Hierarchically structured opportunities, unequal employment experiences and unequal life chances, mediated and transmitted through community and family cultures, produce highly differentiated patterns of response and adaptation. Individuals shape and are shaped by a continuous interaction between themselves and their social and economic environments, so that native personality, disposition and skill are not easily disentangled from behaviour moulded by family culture and inherited social capital (Bourdieu, 1977b; Lamont and Lareau, 1988; Thompson, 1997; Dasgupta, 2010). This interplay between child and family produces big differences in cognitive development between rich and poor by the age of 3, long before formal education can be held responsible for 'gaps' in educational attainment (Goodman and Gregg, 2010). It also forms an individual's horizons and sense of what is possible and desirable for 'people like us' (Hodkinson *et al.*, 1996).

The problematic nature of the debate about social mobility is nowhere more apparent than in the debate about standards. Results are expressed in terms of comparative performance, with each candidate's total marks placed in order along the normal distribution curve. Grades are awarded subsequently, according to a mysterious procedure determined by government agencies and the examiners responsible for each paper. The process of norm referencing means that students are always assessed in relation to one another, not against some absolute standard or set of criteria, and this removes the possibility of comparing one year's cohort with another. Each year, similar proportions of students will achieve better or worse marks than others, however brilliant the teaching and however easy or rigorous the examination, and it is statistically impossible to increase the number of candidates with above-average scores (Barker, 2010).

Grade boundaries have been used to mask this reality, however, so that progressively more candidates have been awarded higher grades. This does not represent improvement but rather a change in the valuation placed on candidates who receive average and above-average marks – which has led to allegations that New Labour administrations facilitated grade inflation (Mansell, 2007, 2011). Qualifications operate as filters for the labour market, so an increased supply of candidates with higher grades must reduce the relative value of GCSEs rather than improve social mobility, unless more high-quality jobs become available.

Gove hopes that appeals to rigour and tradition will fix the problem of inflation but it is inevitable that, when grade boundaries shift in response to perceived improvement, his new 'world class' qualifications will be as vulnerable to the 'falling standards' complaint as those they are replacing. If grade boundaries do not shift, there will be no evidence of improvement in education and no grounds for claiming that schools can increase social mobility. But if more candidates achieve higher grades, the result will be greater competition for available places in higher education and employment, not increased status and rewards for successful students (Brown, 2001). Gove does not seem to have considered the possibility of an over-supply of young people with traditional academic knowledge and interests.

We have serious reservations, therefore, about the coherence and rigour of the Coalition's policy framework, and doubt the practicality of the specific education proposals outlined in *The Importance of Teaching* and *Opening Doors, Breaking Barriers* (DfE, 2010a; HMG, 2011). The government's one-sided, hyper-individualist plans neglect the reality of children's lives and experience, and over-estimate the extent to which cherished reforms can increase the number of young people obtaining higher-status jobs. These reservations, based on close scrutiny of policy documents and the careful reading of a wide range of studies concerned with social mobility and change, were confirmed by analysis of our student interview data.

Our respondents' strategies became intelligible only when we began to draw on a wider variety of concepts. Anna and Elijah illustrate the puzzle at the centre of this book: why do similar educational experiences lead to such different lives? These two students attend the same highly effective school, are equally determined and hard-working, and share a strong sense of personal responsibility for reaching the demanding targets they have been set (see chapter 1). But Anna plans to study childcare at a local college, while Elijah is headed for an elite university. Elijah's potential income from a career in economics, international relations or aeronautical engineering is likely to be many times greater than Anna's earnings in childcare. The analysis (in chapters 3–6) uses the concepts of habitus, field and institutional habitus to interpret respondents' lives, decisions and pathways, and to begin to understand why education leads to such diverse destinations. Our findings are summarized below.

Schools and achievement

2. High-performing schools emphasize excellent teaching, high expectations and achievement. Students believe they are 'authors of their own lives' and work hard to reach challenging goals and targets. They are competitive and accept full responsibility for their own relative success or failure (chapter 3).

Student and teacher interviews, supplemented by additional data from relevant Ofsted reports, provide strong evidence that these conditions are met to a remarkable extent. Felix Holt was found to achieve outstanding outcomes, with 'no significant difference in the progress of different groups of students' (Felix Holt Ofsted report, 2011), while South Park was identified as a 'good' school in 2008 and has demonstrated sustained progress since then (South Park Ofsted interim assessment, 2012). Comments on teaching at Felix Holt were unanimously positive. Those who came to the sixth form from elsewhere emphasized the excellence of Felix Holt's provision compared with the limitations of their previous schools.

Students at South Park strongly identified with their school's community ethos and values, and praised the way 'teachers and pupils are there to help you and take time and trouble' (Emma). There was general enthusiasm for 'really good' teachers (Sharon), with most A and B group members believing that South Park compared favourably with local competitors, including well-known private schools. But a number of students were critical and pointed to marked differences between their 'outstanding' and 'poor' teachers. Driven by challenging, personalized targets, the respondents knew the value of a good teacher and were impatient with average and below-average tuition. The criticism also illustrates how hard it is for schools to sustain consistently high-quality teaching across the curriculum, even in apparently favourable contexts. Success in achieving challenging targets depends on high levels of teaching competence, but these are not easily guaranteed, especially in subjects where there is a shortage of teachers.

Sandy and Gavin (South Park B group) rejected an academic curriculum that seemed irrelevant to their lives and distanced themselves from their teachers and classmates. Sandy complained that South Park was only interested in students who have high grades and felt that French was a 'waste of my time'. Gavin protested that revision was boring and repetitive, saying he was ready to get on with his life. These were the only respondents in our sample to resemble Kenny and Martin, the alienated working-class students described in Reay's (2006) Economic and Social Research Council Project. Their disaffection with South Park suggests that an examination-powered curriculum does not work for everyone, even in good schools serving socially advantaged communities.

Other students interviewed at the two schools seemed comfortable with the demands made on them and emphasized their willingness to work hard to reach their desired college or university place. They viewed the future as 'entirely in my own hands' and saw school as an ideal meritocracy where hard work and application earn their just rewards. Respondents were confident that they could choose and manage their future careers and that social class, ethnicity and gender would not impede their progress, even within relatively obscure or inaccessible areas of employment. They had internalized individualist discourses in which hard work and competitive edge are the keys to successful lives and careers.

Almost every respondent acknowledged the importance of formal examinations and accepted responsibility for their own relative success and failure. With the exception of Sandy and Gavin, students spoke readily about grades and targets, and were willing to adjust their plans should there be significant discrepancies between estimated and actual results. Students' dreams of the future were centred on securing the qualifications necessary to enter their chosen profession; they said there would be no one to blame but themselves if they did not secure the right grades for admission to a desired college, university or vocational pathway.

Overall, the majority of our students presented themselves as astute, highly motivated, and hard-working. Almost all the respondents described clear plans for the future and recognized that they would have to adapt to circumstances, including unfavourable grades. They were acting as the reflexive agents of individualism whose decisions were 'pragmatically rational' (Hodkinson *et al.,* 1996). Their dispositions were aligned with the formal demands and expectations of the examination system, and latent individualism led them to pursue opportunities in competition with their peers (Giddens, 1991). Those with professional parents were influenced by the high-status academic milieu in which they had grown up, while others with parents engaged in vocational careers as plumbers, builders and hairdressers were likely to aspire to similar occupations.

South Park and Felix Holt have adopted a wide range of strategies to improve attainment, including mentoring and target-setting, and their students have responded eagerly to the opportunities provided. Both schools promote high expectations and encourage faith in good grades as a passport to future success. Respondents believed that working hard would enable them to reach their targets. Some saw themselves as competitive and aimed to achieve a measure of status and control in the workplace as well as financial security for their future families. Respondents who had experienced family hardship were also more likely to emphasize the importance of employment that would yield a stable, regular income.

Families and children
3. Family background has less influence than before on student decisions about education and employment. High-performing schools are reducing outcome differences between less-advantaged students and their peers (chapter 4).

Policy-makers have construed family background and circumstances as barriers to be broken down so that poor students can enjoy similar opportunities to their wealthier peers. They envision academies as centres of social engineering, where high expectations and high-quality teaching enable every hard-working and determined person to succeed. This approach is similar to that adopted under New Labour, when policy was designed to change the attitudes and behaviour of 'socially excluded' families, described in formulaic terms as living in 'challenging circumstances' or in 'areas of disadvantage'. Gewirtz (2001: 136) argues that New Labour policy gurus aimed to reconstruct and transform working-class parents into middle-class ones, with excellence for the many to be achieved in part by 'making the many behave like the few'. The Coalition's plan that every child should attend a school as good as the best in the independent sector is based on a similar desire to rescue the less fortunate from their families and immerse them in elite learning and culture.

Our qualitative data offers a contrasting picture of the role of family background, culture and capital in respondents' lives and suggests that these influences can be positive and negative for everyone, not just the disadvantaged. The family is not an independent variable to be overcome but the source of a rich mixture of dispositions that are imprinted through childhood and play a vital part in people's growth, learning and outlook (Bourdieu, 1977a). The family is on the inside of children's development, while the school is on the outside, looking in with a measure of frustration when pupils do not behave as teachers should like them to.

Regardless of background and circumstances, respondents cited countless instances of valued parental support and encouragement, with over 70 per cent referring to help with homework, financial support for trips, or assistance with extracurricular activities and work experience. They acknowledged their parents' expectations of them and emphasized the importance of positive family relationships for their own happiness. Students from poor backgrounds were equally likely to speak positively about their parents' care and attention. Supportive families played an important role in enabling the students to sustain their effort. Our two schools show parents, teachers and students sharing common goals and collaborating effectively to achieve them.

Participants were also eager to claim they were not hindered by poverty, lack of resources or other negative circumstances. They acknowledged personal difficulties but invariably described these as obstacles to be overcome, not as explanations for lack of success. B group members were much more likely to cite examples of redundancy, financial pressure, family break-up, emotional upsets, illness and disability, but they remained optimistic, nevertheless, about their prospects and opportunities. This is consistent with the positive, individualistic attitudes expressed by participants and supports the government's case that good schools can create a climate where students work hard and aim to achieve great results. But it is much less clear that the effects of disadvantage can be overcome. Less successful students at both schools were more likely to assess themselves as 'disadvantaged' and their families were often troubled by financial, emotional and health issues. B group members were also more likely to be following vocational tracks towards less-prestigious employment (see below).

Our data also shows that family background and resources shaped respondents' identities, outlook, values, interests and vocational aspirations. Parental occupations were reported as a significant influence on participants' growing sense of personal status and identity. The majority of South Park A group members, for example, were very much aware of their parents' professional, academic and scientific occupations and regarded themselves as intelligent, capable people. They spoke confidently about their options and careers and assumed they would study at prestigious universities before progressing to high-level, knowledge-based work. Some less-advantaged students identified with mothers or fathers who had overcome redundancy, unemployment and financial difficulties and succeeded too in holding their families together. Other stories of disadvantage led us to conclude that illness and poverty are not incidental misfortunes but formative ingredients in family histories, with long-term consequences for young people's personal development, self-perceptions and life chances.

Students were also strongly influenced by family values, climate and culture. They often attributed their interests, hobbies and activities to family members, including parents, grandparents and other significant relatives. Faith's father introduced her to the local youth drama group and she was now contemplating a career in the performing arts. Isaac's family had always kept animals and he now aspired to work in a pet shop. Our sample provided many examples of rich and diverse family lives that contributed to respondents' values and interests. Family habitus was important, with interests in art (Louise, Andrew), music (Daniel, Richard), languages (Rachael) and sport (Mary, Carl, Jordan) emulated and developed by the next generation.

This data shows that family antecedents, circumstances and networks have a considerable influence on young people's dispositions, and long-term implications for their educational and career trajectories. Our respondents' stories tell of many twists of fortune and illustrate the accumulation of small (and sometimes large) advantages and disadvantages that help and hinder individual progress (Gladwell, 2008). Families play a crucial part in young people's lives, whatever their background, and in many ways form the essential foundations for formal education.

This conclusion is reinforced by the number of students at South Park (33 per cent) and at Felix Holt (40 per cent) who fail to attain the good GCSE threshold (5 A*–C grades, including English and mathematics), despite the excellent systems in place to raise standards and improve performance. The poorer results of this significant minority confirm the expectation that poor children are likely to do badly, even in highly effective schools (Cook, 2012).

Aspirations

4. Students aspire to high-status educational and employment opportunities associated with increased chances of relative social mobility. They seek a degree of power and autonomy in their work, and to accumulate economic security and material advantage (chapter 5).

The Coalition's view of social mobility is driven by economic considerations. Since at least 2001, policy-makers have been convinced that increased mobility 'can drive growth by creating a more highly skilled workforce and putting people in the right jobs for their talents' (HMG, 2011: 11). Economic benefits are said to include a 4 per cent addition to gross domestic product (GDP) and a significant improvement in the underlying growth rate (HMG, 2011). Gove may hope to extend 'the liberating power of a great education to the poorest' (2011a, unpaged) and to free people to become 'authors of their own lives' (DfE, 2010a: 6) but the government's stated objective, nevertheless, is to increase mobility and economic growth.

The neo-liberal assumption behind this stance is that most people wish to get ahead, escape their family backgrounds and improve their relative status and prosperity. If the prototype academies improve standards, raise expectations and open doors, schools like South Park and Felix Holt should yield evidence that young people are aiming to rise above their families to pursue dreams of prestigious employment and a generally better life. We should expect our sample to refer to worldly motives related to a desire for self-improvement and upward mobility.

Although some of our respondents said status and wealth were important for them, our data in general does not confirm the policy assumption that young people are dissatisfied with their lives and families and wish to climb the social and economic ladder. On the contrary, the most frequently voiced areas of aspiration were personal happiness and satisfaction, with family life and intrinsically rewarding work seen as more important to feelings of success and well-being than the pursuit of status and wealth. Noah, for example, commented that 'pay is much less important than enjoyment of the job'. B group members tended to place an even greater emphasis on a happy family life than their A group counterparts, but students from across the sample explained their keen desire to combine pleasing parents and teachers with securing their own independence and happiness.

Our analysis of the interview transcripts identified five frequently-cited areas of aspiration (personal happiness, job satisfaction, making a difference, status, and wealth) and revealed significant links between students' dreams of success and their family habitus and capital. These are reviewed below:

Personal happiness

Participants who expressed a desire for personal happiness seemed anxious to reproduce the happy family conditions they had experienced through their formative years, and very much valued the economic, emotional and educational support provided at home. The social class of their families seemed to influence their thoughts in this area less than the stability, contentment and help that their parents managed to provide.

Policy-makers have paid little attention to the importance of happiness and security in young people's constructions of future career success. They have not acknowledged the extent to which many school students aim to reproduce the comfortable conditions they know, rather than detaching themselves from their families to pursue opportunities for upward mobility.

Job satisfaction

Students frequently linked job satisfaction with personal happiness and stressed their desire to be happy at home and in their work. A and B group members were equally interested in earning sufficient money to be comfortable and do the things they valued, but most said this would constitute success only if they were also happy. This aspiration was more frequently mentioned at Felix Holt, reflecting perhaps the 18-year-olds' greater proximity to the job market and the immediacy of their thoughts about the workplace. Our data suggests that many young people, contrary to official expectations, are far more concerned with working in a challenging, stimulating environment than with improving their personal status.

Making a difference

Female respondents were more likely to say they were seeking work that would enable them to make a positive difference in the world. Zoey put into words desires common to the (mainly female) students who hoped to make a difference: 'As long as I've made a contribution to the world, even if it's tiny, I'll feel I've been successful'. This aspiration is consistent with stereotypical images of 'good girls' who aim to be selfless, caring and nurturing, but also illustrates the limitations of individualist views of the workplace, where everyone is supposed to be motivated by the desire for personal status and advantage (Skelton and Francis, 2009).

Status

Although most respondents referred to diverse goals and desires inconsistent with individualist models of self-help and self-advancement, a small group of male students at South Park said they were pursuing prestigious routes that would lead to status, material advantage and upward mobility. Alaster was highly unusual in stating that he was 'excited by the opportunity of getting into medicine, and the status it will confer ... It's a very different profession from those pursued by my family who are very old fashioned and normal, my Dad's a salesman.' Elijah also said he was aiming for a high level of professional employment, but his chosen goal seems to relate to his parents' example rather than indicating a desire to outperform them. He appears to have decided that a professional career would be appropriate and suitable for someone like him, and so provides a good example of the operation of habitus.

Wealth

A small number of students expressed a desire for wealth and material advantage, but a high proportion of the sample disavowed the pursuit of money as a personal goal, preferring to emphasize happiness and satisfaction. The wish for material gain seems to be linked with a desire for financial security in the future as a consequence of experiencing personal hardship during childhood.

Respondents who were concerned with financial gain resembled those who sought upward mobility and status in believing that success was the result of individual ambition and hard work. They said nothing that suggested they were aware of the role of social and cultural capital and other family advantages in 'getting ahead', but emphasized individual agency as the critical element in becoming successful. Molly, for example, was inspired by the example of Alan Sugar who 'started with nothing' and built up his career through skill and effort. These students believed in the meritocratic possibilities set before them at home and school.

Some young people certainly saw themselves as lone agents whose fate depended on their own efforts. They believed hard work and ability would be rewarded proportionately, and that they could realize their dreams. But although status and wealth were important for some students, few were concerned primarily with individual advantage. Very few were dissatisfied with their family circumstances and lifestyle, and the idea of 'moving on up' in terms of position, status and wealth was almost entirely absent. Vocational aspirations seemed to be embedded in the family environment and to be closely related to academic results.

Our analysis of student aspirations at the two schools shows the inadequacy of government constructions of social mobility and the need for deeper insight into young people's motives and experience.

Choosing the future

5. Students have clear, rational understandings of available options, routes and pathways through secondary and higher education, training and the workplace. Future choices and outcomes are based on 'horizons for action' that transcend disadvantage and family background (chapter 6).

The student perceptions documented in chapters 3, 4 and 5 are mainly encouraging for policy-makers. Respondents saw themselves as hard-working and to some extent competitive. They accepted full responsibility for the future, rejecting the idea that they are constrained by social class, gender or ethnicity, and they were strongly supported by parents who were eager for their success. Tutors were uncompromising in their drive for the best possible grades; they mentor and coach their charges in the search for suitable work experience placements and entrance to highly-rated colleges and universities.

The young people themselves had adopted the language of targets and grades and were confident that with hard work they will achieve their goals. The students were realistic about their 'horizons for action' but said they had formulated 'pragmatically rational' plans to negotiate an appropriate route through the varied academic and vocational options that lie ahead. They expressed relatively firm and straightforward views of where they wished to be in the future but were aware that their dreams might have to be scaled downwards in the light of examination results.

The interviews confirm that Felix Holt and South Park have produced a favourable climate for social mobility, with students, parents and teachers aligned in the pursuit of the best possible grades and jobs. With a handful of exceptions, the young people showed serious commitment to the individualist model of self-help and self-improvement, and expected to realize their dreams for work and family life, provided they worked hard and got the right grades.

Despite this evidence of progress towards equal opportunities, our interviews also provide warning signs that relative social mobility may be hard to improve. Most young people are happy with their family life and have no real desire or aspiration to climb the social ladder towards higher status and wealth (chapter 5). Our respondents aspired mostly to happiness and intrinsic job satisfaction, and their career intentions were in general related to their parents' occupational milieus. In this they resembled participants in Richardson's (1977) study, who were well integrated into their class and community and seemed blinkered in their compliance with family expectations. Our sample contained very few young people who resembled Richardson's upwardly mobile informants, apparently at odds with their environment from early childhood and willing to take risks in challenging and unpredictable conditions.

Although both schools encourage everyone to fulfil their potential, outcomes remain closely related to family background and expectations, with a substantial minority of students overall failing to attain the good GCSE threshold (see chapter 4). The students' academic orientation and work preferences seemed to be related closely to their family habitus and dispositions, with those from a professional milieu contemplating university and middle-class occupations, while others from manual backgrounds seemed content to apply for the vocational courses needed to enter the local economy, perhaps as a plumber, hairdresser or a shopkeeper.

Family patterns and influences played an important role in shaping young people's plans for the workplace. The concept of economic, social and cultural capital, transmitted through families, helps make sense of the difference between academic and vocational-track students, and suggests that mobility really is 'as much a matter of family praxis as individual agency' (Bourdieu, 1977a; Bertaux and Thompson, 1997: 7).

These family dispositions were reinforced by the tracking systems operated at both new academies. All 24 A group students at South Park were committed to the 'high academic' track, with Oxbridge and other Russell Group universities in their sights. By contrast, B group respondents were already adapting to less-prestigious and generally vocational ambitions. A similar marked contrast between the academic and employment paths pursued by A and B group members was observed at Felix Holt. All but one of the A group were headed for high-status universities, while B group students spanned the 'academic' and 'vocational' tracks.

Students find themselves on parallel but distinct tracks, with contrasting curricula and examinations that lead towards dissimilar occupational destinations. Internal school processes (curriculum structures, assessment, and guidance) seem to shape students' aspirations and expectations, sorting and labelling them for a stable job market rather than preparing them for new challenges. The design of public examinations ensures that education, regardless of its quality and intrinsic value to students, serves to distribute rather than enlarge available opportunities, and contributes to social stability rather than upward mobility. This is because students are rewarded for their position on the normal distribution curve, not for their skills and abilities, however valuable (see chapter 2).

There are many immensely able students at South Park and Felix Holt who are set to gain outstanding grades. It is too soon, however, to judge the extent to which their academic credentials will translate into upward mobility, or to predict an individual's success in seizing future opportunities and climbing an occupational ladder. There is clear potential, however, for bright A group students at both schools to secure above-average earnings and future mobility. But this potential may not be realized in the difficult economic environment that has followed the 2007 credit crunch and subsequent banking crisis. Young people from professional, double-income families may struggle to match their parents' acquisition of resources. These students may obtain better qualifications than previous generations of their families, but increased participation at all levels of education means that advantaged students have to secure very strong credentials to maintain their family's position, let alone to better it.

The Felix Holt Family Employment History (see chapter 6 and Appendix 2) provides patchy but significant evidence that families, rather than individuals, are the appropriate unit of analysis for studies in social mobility. Students are not isolated individuals in simple pursuit of ever more prestigious credentials, but contributors to evolving family patterns and networks that produce advantages or disadvantages for successive generations. We need to examine family case studies closely to understand the ways in which parents and other relatives contribute to the transmission of skills and resources, and families adapt to opportunities occurring in their local environment (Bertaux and Thompson, 1997).

The Family Employment History also suggests the web of family connections and resources that influence young people's academic and vocational choices, and reveals the limitations of studies concerned exclusively with male earnings. Changes in the labour market have made women ever more important players in the household economy and have provided greatly improved opportunities for young women today compared with their mothers and grandmothers. Women now play a vital part in the social and economic standing of their families. This increases the need to assess women's contributions to social mobility.

Dream or reality

The evidence from our 'best case' social mobility study leads us to conclude that government expectations for school reform are unduly optimistic. Our data provides no evidence that high-performance schools create favourable conditions for upward mobility, and confirms the strength of family, community and wider social/economic influences.

This helps us to understand the paradox that a huge expansion in educational opportunity in the last 25 years has coincided with a marked increase in inequality and a reduction in the number of jobs that involve high levels of skill. Professional and skilled work has become more standardized, more routine, and less well paid, despite a great increase in the annual cohort of highly qualified graduates. It seems that most of what we take for educational improvement is in effect credentialing, i.e. a change in the terms of social competition between variously equipped groups (Goldthorpe, 1987; Brown, 2001). Education is not an external catalyst but an intrinsic part of the social complexity that leads to unequal outcomes of the kind documented in government reports.

We argue that upward mobility is either reserved for an exceptional few with pre-existing advantages (and so consists of the replacement of one elite with another), or dependent on economic expansion, driven by millions of students acquiring profitable new skills and earning new status within a much less steep social gradient. The first scenario does not seem to improve social justice, except for a select few, while there is strong historic evidence that the second may be desirable but is unattainable, especially at a time when inequality and disadvantage are increasing.

Our interviews suggest that individualist conceptions of social mobility are inadequate and encourage a mistaken focus on talented, determined individuals, rather than serious attention to the complex social processes at work. We argue that future policy should stress qualitative research that increases our understanding of the role of families (including women), of the ways in which dispositions are formed and sustained, and of the occupational patterns to which individuals belong.

Our study also contributes an unexpected insight into the failure of the sociological imagination. Individualist ideas persist, despite their many, obvious limitations, because people very often fail to see beyond their own limited and particular circumstances. Our students did not talk of a pattern, only of their own agency, apparently unaware of the structured constraints that might limit them, and were eager to embrace an individualist perspective. They showed little knowledge of the work undertaken by their grandparents, and sometimes knew little about the work reality even of their own parents. They do not perceive the degree to which their lives are shaped by the transmission of family resources and dispositions, and by the opportunities of their own time and place.

Appendix 1: South Park Student Tracks

Student	Group	Background	Aspiration	Est. grd.	Tr.
Adam	A	Advantaged	Science, leadership	A*	HA
Alaster	A	Average	Medicine	A*	HA
Chloe	A	Middling, academic	Medicine	A*	HA
Clare	A	Advantaged	Child psychology	A*	HA
Elijah	A	Advantaged, ps prof./researcher	Specialized, technical	A*	HA
Ellie	A	Advantaged, ps teach	Not sure, history, English	A*	HA
Emma	A	Average, mum illness	Teacher	A*	HA
Faith	A	Advantaged, mum teacher	Drama teacher, acting	A*	HA
Grace	A	Normal, autistic brother	History, unsure where it leads	A*	HA
Hannah	A	Advantaged, mum teacher	Medicine	A*	HA
Ian	A	Advantaged, ps musicians	Sciences	A*	HA
Isabella	A	Advantaged, ps scientists	Sports medicine	A*	HA
Jacob	A	Advantaged, ps scientists	Not sure of subject	A*	HA
Jason	A	Advantaged	Maths, art	A*	HA
Lily	A	Advantaged, ps academic	SEN, psychology	A*	HA
Mark	A	Average	Medicine	A*	HA
Noah	A	Average	Sports journalism	A*	HA
Oliver	A	Advantaged	Physiotherapy (Nottingham)	A*	HA
Owen	A	Advantaged, ps scientists	Science/maths	A*	HA

Student	Group	Background	Aspiration	Est. grd.	Tr.
Richard	A	Average, ps split	Musical, not sure of subject	A*	HA
Rose	A	PhD/researcher/ teacher	Research at Cambridge	A*	HA
Sean	A	Advantaged, ps profs	High level study	A*	HA
Sophie	A	Average	History teacher	A*	HA
Zoey	A	Advantaged, ps scientists	PhD research	A*	HA
Gabriella	B	Average	Engineering, REME	B	A
Jasmine	B	Advantaged	SEN teacher	B	A
Leah	B	Sick brother, ps can't work	Attendance issues, depression	B	A
Julian	B	Advantaged p (teacher)	Police or sports science	A/B	A/V
Max	B	Dad nurse, homeless	Charity, living abroad	C/D	C
Nathan	B	Technician/social worker	Film director; maths grade may block uni	C/D	C
Alice	B	Average, ps div., bereaved	Course for uniformed services	E	V
Alison	B	Average, ps div., upset	Sport psychology dip.	B/C	V
Anna	B	Disadvantaged, large family	Child care course level 2	D	V
Carl	B	Less prosperous, ps div.	Football coaching	C	V
Cathy	B	Average, mother artist	Art-related job	C	V
Freddie	B	Money tight, ps div.	Professional cookery dip.	C/B	V
Gary	B	Money tight, few holidays	Navy chef	C	V
Gavin	B	Less advantaged, ps div.	Dip. public service, police	D	V

Student	Group	Background	Aspiration	Est. grd.	Tr.
Isaac	B	Decorator/cleaner	Animal management, pet shop	C/D	V
Jordan	B	Money short, ps div.	Sport/leisure course, professional football	E	V
Patrick	B	Comfortable	Plumber	C	V
Ross	B	Property developer/ pharmacist	Sport diploma	C	V
Samantha	B	Advantaged	Photography or health and social care	C	V
Sandy	B	Landscape gardener/hair salon	Hairdressing	D	V
Sebastian	B	Ps own companies	Dyslexia, animal care or radio dip.	E	V
Sharon	B	Comfortable	Health and social care	C/D	V

Key	
Est. grd.	Estimated typical grades
Tr.	Curriculum track
ps	Parents
dip.	Diploma
REME	Royal Electrical and Mechanical Engineers
prof.	professor
div.	divorced
HA	High academic
A	Academic
C	Creative
V	Vocational

Appendix 2: Felix Holt Family Employment History

Student	Grp	Gfather (P)	Gfather (M)	Gmother (P)	Gmother (M)	Father	Mother	Own hope	Grd.	Trk.
Adele	A	RAF pilot	Milkman		Carer/cleaner	Accountant	Carer (OU degree)	Lawyer	A	HA
Andrew	A	Mechanic	Eng.			Carpenter	Illustrator, artist	Wildlife photographer	A	C/A
Ben	A		Military		Housewife	Car sales/driver	Nurse	Education or research	A	A
Charlotte	A	Trade mgr.		Bakery assistant	Cleaner	Trade mgr.	Teaching assistant	Drama teacher	A	A
Colin	A	Farmer	Electrician		Nurse	Clothes company	Confectionery industry	Electronic eng.	A	A
Gemma	A	Eng.	Owned butchers	Support worker	Unknown	Comp. eng.	Support worker	Veterinary surgeon	A	HA
Graham	A	Builder				Insurance mgr.	School admissions	Software developer	A	HA
Jack	A	Mechanic	Owned motor bus.	Car firm	Sweet shop	Accountant, partner	Accountant, part-time	Chemist/research	A	HA
Kylie	A	Miner	Car mechanic			Drainage eng.	Comms. mgr.	Teaching	A	A
Lance	A	Telecoms eng.	Typewriter mechanic	Tailoress	Clerk	Telecoms	Teaching assistant	Electronic eng.	A	A
Lucy	A	Stroke age 30	Phone co. mgr.	Cared for husb.	Sweet factory	Printer, unemployed	BT mgr.	English degree	A	HA
Martin	A	Restaurateur	Lorry driver	Rice fields		Chef	Hairdresser	English degree	A	HA
Michael	A	Wholesale delivery	Engineering	Wholesale office	Electrical testing	Wholesale delivery	Shop work	Electrical eng.	A	HA

Student	Grp	Gfather (P)	Gfather (M)	Gmother (P)	Gmother (M)	Father	Mother	Own hope	Grd.	Trk.
Paul	A	Train driver	Market stall holder		Seamstress	TV sport producer	Teaching assistant	Teacher	A	HA
Rachael	A	Carpenter	Painter	Gardener		Investment banker	Investment banker	Work abroad/ languages	A	HA
Rebecca	A	Headteacher	Carpenter/ salesman	Teacher	Nurse	Mgr. director/ own co.	Teacher	Cancer research	A	HA
Rob	A	Policeman				IT/redundant	Pre-school teacher	Research chemist	A	HA
Tom	A					Manual work	Customer service	Undecided	A	A
Claudia	B	Property developer		Factory worker	Self-employed	Police officer	Admin worker	Primary teacher	B	A
Craig	B					Management	Banker	Artistic	C	C/A
Daniel	B	Farm work	Farm work			Electronic repairs	Teacher	Music technology	C/D	C
Darren	B	Security alarms			Sales assistant	Unknown	Sales assistant	Personal trainer	C/D	V/A
Dave	B	Bank mgr.	Army, milkman	Garden centre	Receptionist	Police sergeant	Nurse/ receptionist	Police	C	V
Dean	B				Child minder		School secretary	Advertising/ marketing	C	V/A
Emilio	B					Administration	Midwife	Geography- related	C	A

Student	Grp	Gfather (P)	Gfather (M)	Gmother (P)	Gmother (M)	Father	Mother	Own hope	Grd.	Trk.
Harry	B					Driving instructor	Tesco main office	Tesco	BTEC	V
Holly	B				Hairdresser	Electrician	Embroiderer	Zoo-keeper	C	V/A
Joyce	B	Lawyer, Ghana	Physicist/ patents	Housework	Art teacher	Building mgr.	Customer service	Groom, equine studies	C	V/A
Lauren	B			Midwife, lecturer		Police officer	Payroll manager	Chemist	B	A
Layla	B		Carpenter	Housewife	Housewife	Bus. transport	Teacher	Trader	C/D	V
Louise	B		Train driver/ taxi co.		Shop assistant	'Drew a lot'	Teaching assistant	Artist	B/A	C/A
Marilyn	B	Window fitter	Factory worker	Care home staff	Teacher	Managing director	School office	Lawyer	A/C	A
Mary	B		Architect	Small co. in US	Worked at Diageo	Comp. tech/ own bus.	Accountant for husb.	Physiotherapy	A/B	V/A
Matt	B		University lecturer			Self-employed builder	House carer	Bus. (big co.)	C/B	A
Mia	B			Nurse		Software developer	Exam invigilator	Journalist/ historian	A/C	A
Molly	B					Own CCTV co.	Works with husb.	Not decided	C/D	C/V
Nick	B	Aero designer	Farmer			Eng.	Eng.	Self-employment	C/D	V

155

Student	Grp	Gfather (P)	Gfather (M)	Gmother (P)	Gmother (M)	Father	Mother	Own hope	Grd.	Trk.
Paula	B	Eng.	Eng.	Housework	Cashier	Carpenter	Teaching assistant	Teacher	B/C	A
Simon	B	Photographer	Estate agent	Nurse	Nurse	Builder	Sales assistant	Media producer	C	V
Tania	B	Merchant navy		Own launderette		Boat builder	Doctor's receptionist	Vet/conservation	B	HA
Tony	B		Water board	Secretary	Paramedic	Accountant	Book-keeper	Accountant	C	V
Zara	B		Army doctor			Construction, builder	Clergy	Lawyer, own bus.	B/A	A

KEY

Column A	Student	Student pseudonym
Column B	Grp	Group A or B
Column C–F	Gfather/mother	Grandparent
	P/M	Paternal/Maternal
Column G–H	Father/mother	
Column I	Own Hope	
Column J	Grd.	Predicted grade/s given by student

Column K		Trk.	Track		
					HA = High academic
					A = Academic
					C = Creative
					V = Vocational
					C/A, C/V, V/A = mixed
				bus.	Business
				co.	Company
				comp.	Computer
				eng.	Engineer
				husb.	Husband
				mgr.	Manager

References

Acker, J. (1973) 'Women and social stratification: A case of intellectual sexism'. *The American Journal of Sociology*, 78 (4), 936–45.

Adonis, A. (2012) *Education, Education, Education: Reforming England's schools.* London: Biteback Publishing.

Allen, M. and Ainley, P. (2010) *Lost Generation? New strategies for youth and education.* London: Continuum International Publishing Group.

Aldridge, S. (2001) *Social Mobility: a discussion paper.* London: Cabinet Office, Performance and Innovation Unit.

Andorka, R. (1997) 'Social mobility in Hungary since the Second World War: Interpretations through surveys and through families' histories'. In Bertaux, D. and Thompson, P. (eds) *Pathways to Social Class: A qualitative approach to social mobility.* Oxford: Clarendon Press, 259–98.

Archer, L., Mendick, H. and Hollingworth, S. (2010) *Urban Youth and Schooling.* Maidenhead: Open University Press.

Arnot, M. (2002) *Reproducing Gender: Essays on educational theory and feminist politics.* London: Routledge Falmer.

Arrow, K., Bowles, S. and Durlauf, S. (eds) (2000) *Meritocracy and Economic Inequality.* Princeton, NJ: Princeton University Press.

Atkinson, W. (2012) 'Reproduction revisited: comprehending complex educational trajectories'. *The Sociological Review*, 60, 735–53.

Ball, S. (2003a) *Class Strategies and the Education Market: The middle class and social advantage.* London: Routledge Falmer.

— (2003b) 'The teacher's soul and the terrors of performativity'. *Journal of Education Policy*, 18 (2), 215–28.

Ball, S., Maguire, M. and Macrae, S. (2000) *Choice, Pathways and Transitions Post-16: New youth, new economies in the global city.* London: Routledge Falmer.

Barber, M. (2008) *Instruction to Deliver: Fighting to transform Britain's public services.* London: Methuen.

Barker, B. (2010a) 'Can education overcome disadvantage?'. *Secondary Headship*, 87, September, 8–9.

— (2010b) *The Pendulum Swings: Transforming school reform.* Stoke on Trent: Trentham Books.

— (2011) 'Can schools change society?' *Forum*, 53 (1), 163–70.

— (2012) 'Frozen pendulum'. *Journal of Educational Administration and History*, 44 (1), 65–88.

— (2013) 'Review: Education Select Committee Report'. *The House*, 36, 1444, 28 February, 12–13.

BBC News (2000) 'Chancellor attacks Oxford admissions'. 26 May. Online. http://news.bbc.co.uk/1/hi/education/764141.stm (accessed 10 May 2013).

— (2008) 'Rise in women doctors "worrying"'. 3 April. Online. http://news.bbc.co.uk/1/hi/health/7329082.stm (accessed 13 June 2012).

— (2012a) 'News: League Tables 2011'. Online. www.bbc.co.uk/news/education-11950098 (accessed 14 November 2012).

— (2012b) 'Pupil premium being used to plug budget cuts, say heads'. 1 May. Online. www.bbc.co.uk/news/education-17909023 (accessed 6 June 2012).

— (2013a) 'Debt worries feature payday loans, says StepChange'. 7 May. Online. www.bbc.co.uk/news/business-22436306 (accessed 19 June 2013).

— (2013b) '"Invisible" poor children let down by schools, says Ofsted head'. 20 June. Online. www.bbc.co.uk/news/education-22970674 (accessed 20 June 2013).

BBC Science (2013) 'The Great British Class Survey – Results'. 3 April. Online. www.bbc.co.uk/science/0/21970879 (accessed 17 May 2013).

Beckmann, A. and Cooper, C. (2005) 'Conditions of domination: reflections on harms generated by the British state education system'. *British Journal of Sociology of Education*, 26 (4), 475–90.

BERA (2011) Ethical Guidelines for Educational Research. Online. www.bera.ac.uk/system/files/3/BERA-Ethical-Guidelines-2011.pdf (accessed 22 August 2013).

Bernstein, B. (1970) 'Education cannot compensate for society'. *New Society*, 389, 26 February, 344–7.

— (1971) *Theoretical Studies Towards a Sociology of Language*. London: Routledge. Vol. 1 of *Class, Codes and Control*. 2 vols. 1971–3.

Bertaux, D. (1997) 'Transmission in extreme situations: Russian families expropriated by the October Revolution'. In Bertaux, D. and Thompson, P. (eds) *Pathways to Social Class: A qualitative approach to social mobility*. Oxford: Clarendon Press, 230–58.

Bertaux, D. and Thompson, P. (1997) 'Introduction'. In Bertaux, D. and Thompson, P. (eds) *Pathways to Social Class: A qualitative approach to social mobility*. Oxford: Clarendon Press, 1–31.

Bertaux, D. and Thompson, P. (eds) (1997) *Pathways to Social Class: A qualitative approach to social mobility*. Oxford: Clarendon Press.

Blair, T. (2002) 'Full text of Tony Blair's speech on welfare reform'. In *The Guardian* 10 June. Online. www.guardian.co.uk/society/2002/jun/10/socialexclusion.politics1 (accessed 5 June 2013).

Blanden, J. and Machin, S. (2008) 'Up and down the generational income ladder in Britain: past changes and future prospects'. *National Institute Economic Review*, 205 (1), 101–16. Online. http://ner.sagepub.com/content/205/1/101 (accessed 14 April 2012) (requires subscription).

Blanden, J., Gregg, P. and Machin, S. (2005a) *Intergenerational Mobility in Europe and North America*. London: Centre for Economic Performance, London School of Economics.

— (2005b) 'Social mobility in Britain: low and falling'. *CentrePiece*, Spring, 18–20. Online. http://cep.lse.ac.uk/centrepiece/ (accessed 15 April 2012).

Blanden, J., Machin, S., Goodman, A. and Gregg, P. (2002) 'Changes in intergenerational mobility in Britain'. Paper presented at the Annual Conference of the British Educational Research Association, University of Exeter, 12–14 September. Online. www.leeds.ac.uk/educol/documents/00002425.htm (accessed 11 April 2012).

Blunkett, D. (2008) *The Inclusive Society: Social mobility in 21ˢᵗ century Britain*. London: Progress.

Boudon, R. (1974) *Education, Opportunity and Social Inequality*. New York: Wiley.

Bourdieu, P. (1977a) *Outline of a Theory of Practice*. Cambridge: Cambridge University Press.

— (1977b) 'Cultural Reproduction and Social Reproduction'. In Karabel, J. and Halsey, A. (eds) *Power and Ideology in Education*. Oxford: Oxford University Press, 487–511.

— (1986) 'The forms of capital'. Trans. Nice, R. In Richardson, J. (ed.), *Handbook of Theory of Research for the Sociology of Education*. New York: Greenwood Press, 241–58.

— (1990) *The Logic of Practice*. Cambridge: Polity.

— (1993a) *Sociology in Question*. London: Sage.

— (1993b) 'Concluding remarks: for a sociogenetic understanding of intellectual works'. In Calhoun, C., LiPuma, E. and Postone, M. (eds) *Bourdieu: Critical Perspectives*. Cambridge: Polity, 263–75.

Bourdieu, P. and Passeron, J-C. (1977) *Reproduction in Education, Society and Culture*. London: Sage.

Brah, A. and Phoenix, A. (2004) 'Ain't I a Woman? Revisiting intersectionality'. *Journal of International Women's Studies,* 5 (3), 75–86.

Breen, R. (1997) 'Inequality, economic growth and social mobility'. *The British Journal of Sociology*, 48 (3), 429–49.

Bright, M. (2005) 'The politics column – Martin Bright revisits the great education divide'. *New Statesman* 31 October. Online. www.newstatesman.com/node/151876 (accessed 11 April 2007).

Broecke, S. and Hamed, J. (2008) *Gender Gaps in Higher Education Participation: An analysis of the relationship between prior attainment and young participation by gender, socio-economic class and ethnicity*. DIUS Research Report 08-14. Department for Innovation, Universities and Skills. Online. www.dius.gov.uk/research (accessed 7 June 2012).

Brown, D. (2001) 'The social sources of educational credentialism: status cultures, labor markets, and organizations'. *Sociology of Education*, 74, Extra issue: 'Current of Thought: Sociology of Education at the Dawn of the 21st Century', 19–34.

Bunting, M. (2009) 'Again social evils haunt Britain. Do we still have the spirit to thwart them?' In *The Guardian* 15 June. Online. www.theguardian.com/commentisfree/2009/jun/14/society-community-uk-morality (accessed 30 March 2013).

Cabinet Office Strategy Unit (2008) '*Getting On, Getting Ahead. A discussion paper: analysing the trends and drivers of social mobility*'. Online. http://dera.ioe.ac.uk/8835/ (accessed 14 April 2012).

Calhoun, C., LiPuma, E. and Postone, M. (eds) (1993) *Bourdieu: Critical perspectives*. Cambridge: Polity.

Carvel, J. (2000) 'Poverty no excuse for failure, says Blunkett'. *The Guardian* 2 March. Online. www.guardian.co.uk/uk/2000/mar/02/schools.news1 (accessed 13 May 2013).

Channel 4 News (2010) 'Budget 2010: welfare benefits cut'. 22 June 2010. Online. www.channel4.com/news/articles/uk/budget+2010+welfare+benefits+cut/3688032.html (accessed 21 June 2011).

Childs, D. (2006) *Britain Since 1945: A political history*. Originally 2001. Abingdon: Routledge.

Chowdry, H. and Sibieta, L. (2011) *Trends in Education and Schools Spending*. Institute for Fiscal Studies, Briefing Note BN121. Online. www.ifs.org.uk/bns/bn121.pdf (accessed 14 July 2012).

Clifton, J. (2011) 'The Independent View: Coalition's social mobility strategy failing'. In *Liberal Democrat Voice*, 28 October. Online. www.libdemvoice.org/the-independent-view-coalitions-social-mobility-strategy-failing-25709.html (accessed 15 April 2012).

Coats, M. (1994) *Women's Education*. Buckingham: Open University Press.

Collins, R. (1981) 'Crises and declines in credentialing systems'. In Collins, R. (ed.) *Sociology since Mid-Century*. New York: Academic Press, 191–215.

Comaroff, J. and Comaroff, J.L. (2001) 'Millennial capitalism: First thoughts on a second coming'. In Comaroff, J. and Comaroff, J.L. (eds) *Millennial Capitalism and the Culture of Neoliberalism*. Durham, NC: Duke University Press, 1–56.

Connell, R. (2005) *Masculinities*. Berkeley: University of California Press.

Contini, G. (1997) 'The local world view: social change and memory in three Tuscan communes'. In Bertaux, D. and Thompson, P. (eds) *Pathways to Social Class: A qualitative approach to social mobility*. Oxford: Clarendon Press, 183–97.

Cook, C. (2012) 'The social mobility challenge for school reformers'. *FT Data* 22 February. Online. http://blogs.ft.com/ftdata/2012/02/22/social-mobility-and-schools/#axzz1o06SJkBJ (registration required) (accessed 11 March 2012).

Crawford, C., Johnson, P., Machin, S. and Vignoles, A. (2011) *Social Mobility: A literature review*. London: Department for Business, Innovation and Skills.

Crozier, G., Reay, D., James, D., Jamieson, F., Beedell, P., Hollingworth, S. and Williams, K. (2008) 'White middle-class parents, identities, educational choice and the urban comprehensive school: dilemmas, ambivalence and moral ambiguity'. *British Journal of Sociology of Education*, 29 (3), 261–72.

Dasgupta, P. (2010) *Partha Dasgupta interviewed by Alan Macfarlane 6th April (part 2)*. Video podcast and transcript retrieved from www.alanmacfarlane.com/DO/filmshow/dasgupta2_fast.htm (accessed 10 April 2013).

Datablog (2012) 'How have GCSE pass rates changed over the exams' 25 year history?' *The Guardian* 17 September. Online. www.guardian.co.uk/news/datablog/2012/sep/17/gcse-exams-replaced-ebacc-history-pass-rates (accessed 18 July 2013).

Debrett (2010) *Debrett's Peerage & Baronetage*. Suffolk: Debrett's.

Deem, R. (1981) 'State policy and ideology in the education of women, 1944–1980'. *British Journal of Sociology of Education*, 2 (2), 131–43.

Department for Education (DfE) (2010a) *The Importance of Teaching: The schools white paper*. London: The Stationery Office.

— (2010b) *The Importance of Teaching: White paper equalities impact assessment* (CM-7980). London: The Stationery Office. Online. www.gov.uk/government/publications/the-importance-of-teaching-the-schools-white-paper-2010 (accessed 19 May 2013).

— (2013a) *The National Curriculum in England: Framework document for consultation*. Online. http://media.education.gov.uk/assets/files/pdf/n/national%20curriculum%20consultation%20-%20framework%20document.pdf (accessed 5 June 2013).

— (2013b) *Draft National Curriculum programmes of study for KS4 English, maths and science*. Online. www.education.gov.uk/schools/teachingandlearning/curriculum/nationalcurriculum2014/a00220610/draft-pos-ks4-english-maths-science (accessed 7 June 2013).

Department for Education and Department for Business, Innovation & Skills (2011) *Wolf Report: Review of vocational education*. Online. www.gov.uk/government/publications/review-of-vocational-education-the-wolf-report (accessed 15 August 2013).

Deputy Prime Minister (DPM's Office) (2011) *Attainment at age 16 by free school meal eligibility*. Online. www.dpm.cabinetoffice.gov.uk/content/attainment-age-16-free-school-meal-eligibility (accessed 17 March 2013).

Devine, F. (2004) *Class Practices: How parents help their children get good jobs*. Cambridge: Cambridge University Press.

Diefenbach, T. and Sillince, J. (2009) 'Hierarchical order in different organisational forms'. Paper presented at the 15th World Congress of the International Industrial Relations Association, Sydney, Australia, August. Online. www.ilera-directory.org/15thworldcongress/files/papers/Track_1/Tue_P1_Diefenbach.pdf (accessed 23 June 2013).

DiMaggio, P. (1982) 'Cultural capital and school success: the impact of status culture participation on the grades of U.S. high school students'. *American Sociological Review*, 47 (2), 189–201.

Dyhouse, C. (1995) *No Distinction of Sex? Women in British universities*. London: Routledge.

Equality Trust (2012) *Research Digest No. 4: Social mobility*. London: The Equality Trust. Online. www.equalitytrust.org.uk/sites/default/files/research-digest-social-mobility-final.pdf (accessed 3 March 2013).

Erikson, R. and Goldthorpe, J. (2010) 'Has social mobility in Britain decreased? Reconciling divergent findings on income and class mobility'. *The British Journal of Sociology*, 61 (2), 211–30.

Ermisch, J. (2008) 'Origins of social immobility and inequality: parenting and early child development'. National Institute Economic Review, 205 (1), 62–71. Online. http://ner.sagepub.com/content/205/1/62 (requires subscription) (accessed 14 April 2012).

Ermisch, J. and Francesconi, M. (2002) *Intergenerational Social Mobility and Assortative Mating in Britain*. IZA Discussion Paper No. 465. Institute for Social and Economic Research, University of Essex and IZA, Bonn.

Eysenck, H. (1971) *Race, Intelligence and Education: Towards a new society*. London: Maurice Temple Smith.

Feldman, M., Otto, S., and Christiansen, F. (2000) 'Genes, culture and inequality'. In Arrow, K., Bowles, S. and Durlauf, S. (eds) *Meritocracy and Economic Inequality*. Princeton, NJ: Princeton University Press, 61–85.

Felix Holt Ofsted report, 2011 – Full reference details withheld to safeguard participant identities.

Flannery, K. and Marcus, J. (2012) *The Creation of Inequality: How our prehistoric ancestors set the stage for monarchy, slavery and empire*. Cambridge, MA: Harvard University Press.

Foot, M. (1962) *Aneurin Bevan: A biography, vol. 1: 1897–1945*. London: MacGibbon and Kee. Vol. 1 of *Aneurin Bevan: A biography*. 2 vols. 1962–1974. London: MacGibbon and Kee.

Francis, B. (2000) *Boys, Girls and Achievement: Addressing the classroom issues*. London: Routledge Falmer.

Furlong, A. and Biggart, A. (1999) 'Framing "choices": a longitudinal study of occupational aspirations among 13- to 16-year-olds'. *Journal of Education and Work*, 12 (1), 21–35.

Gaine, C. (1995) *Still No Problem Here*. Stoke on Trent: Trentham Books.

George, R. (2010) 'Inner city girls: choosing schools and negotiating friendships'. In Jackson, C., Paechter, C. and Renold, E. (2010) *Girls and Education 3–16: continuing concerns, new agendas*. Maidenhead: Open University Press, 91–103.

Gewirtz, S. (2001) 'Cloning the Blairs: New Labour's programme for the re-socialization of working-class parents'. *Journal of Education Policy*, 16 (4), 365–78.

Gewirtz, S. and Ball, S. (2000) 'From "welfarism" to "new managerialism": shifting discourses of school headship in the education marketplace'. *Discourse: Studies in the Cultural Politics of Education*, 21 (3), 253–68.

Giddens, A. (1991) *Modernity and Self-Identity*. Cambridge: Polity Press.

Gladwell, M. (2008) *Outliers: The story of success*. New York: Little, Brown.

Goldstein, H. (2001) 'Using pupil performance data for judging schools and teachers: scope and limitations'. *British Educational Research Journal*, 27 (4), 433–43.

Goldstein, H. and Thomas, S. (1996) 'Using examination results as indicators of school and college performance'. *Journal of the Royal Statistical Society*, 159 (1), 149–63.

Goldthorpe, J. (1987) *Social Mobility and Class Structure in Modern Britain*. Oxford: Clarendon Press.

— (1996) 'Class analysis and the reorientation of class theory: the case of persisting differentials in educational attainment'. *The British Journal of Sociology*, 47 (3), 481–505.

Goldthorpe, J. and Jackson, M. (2007) 'Intergenerational class mobility in contemporary Britain: political concerns and empirical findings'. *The British Journal of Sociology*, 58 (4), 525–46.

Goldthorpe, J. and Mills, C. (2008) 'Trends in intergenerational class mobility in modern Britain: evidence from national surveys, 1972–2005'. *National Institute Economic Review*, 205 (1), 83–100. Online. http://ner.sagepub.com/content/205/1/83 (accessed 14 April 2012).

Goodman, A. and Gregg, P. (eds) (2010) *Poorer Children's Educational Attainment: How important are attitudes and behaviour?* York: Joseph Rowntree Foundation.

Gorard, S. (2008) 'A re-consideration of rates of "social mobility" in Britain: or why research impact is not always a good thing'. *The British Journal of Sociology of Education*, 29 (3), 317–24.

Gottfredson, L. (2002) 'Gottfredson's theory of circumscription, compromise, and self-creation'. In Brown, D. and associates (eds) *Career Choice and Development: Fourth edition*, San Francisco: Jossey Bass, 85–148.

Gove, M. (2011a) 'The moral purpose of school reform'. Address at the National College for School Leadership, Birmingham, 16 June. Online. www.education. gov.uk/inthenews/speeches/a0077859/the-moral-purpose-of-school-reform (accessed 22 March 2013).

— (2011b) 'Oral statement on the schools White Paper'. Department for Education, 9 February. Retrieved from www.education.gov.uk/schools/toolsandinitiatives/ schoolswhitepaper/a0068680/oral-statement (accessed 14 March 2013).

— (2012) 'A coalition for good – how we can all work together to make opportunity more equal'. Speech at Brighton College, 10 May. Retrieved from www. education.gov.uk/inthenews/speeches/a00208822/brighton-college (accessed 12 March 2013).

— (2013) 'I refuse to surrender to the Marxist teachers hell-bent on destroying our schools: Education Secretary berates '"the new enemies of promise'" for opposing his plans'. *Daily Mail* 23 March. Online. http://preview.tinyurl.com/phtk2pm (accessed 27 March 2013).

Gray, J., Jesson, D. and Sime, N. (1995) 'Estimating differences in examination performances of secondary schools in six LEAs: a multi-level approach to school effectiveness'. In Gray, J. and Wilcox, B. (eds) *Good School, Bad School: Evaluating performance and encouraging improvement*. Buckingham: Open University Press, 105–29.

Gregg, P. and Macmillan, L. (2009) *Family Income and Education in the Next Generation: Exploring income gradients in education for current cohorts of youth*. Working Paper No. 09/223, Bristol: Centre for Market and Public Organisation.

Guardian, The (2011) 'Independent schools' GCSE results'. In *The Guardian*. Online. http://education.guardian.co.uk/gcses/table/0,16426,1561652,00.html (accessed 15 July 2013).

Gunter, H. (ed.) (2011) *The State and Education Policy: The Academies programme*. London: Routledge.

Hargreaves, D. (1982) *The Challenge for the Comprehensive School*. London: Routledge & Kegan Paul.

Harrison, J. (2010) *Robert Owen and the Owenites in Britain and America*. Originally 1969. London: Routledge.

Harvey, D. (2005) *A Brief History of Neoliberalism*. Oxford: Oxford University Press.

Hayes, C. (2012) *Twilight of the Elites: America after meritocracy*. New York: Crown Publishers.

Heath, A. and Payne, C. (2000) 'Social mobility'. In Halsey, A. with Webb, J. (eds) *Twentieth Century British Social Trends*. London: Macmillan, 254–78.

Henkel, M. (2005) 'Academic identity and autonomy in a changing policy environment'. *Higher Education*, 49, 155–76.

Henry, J. (2013) 'Brightest pupils failed by state schools, chief inspector warns'. *The Telegraph* 23 June. Online. www.telegraph.co.uk/news/9828734/Brightest-pupils-failed-by-state-schools-chief-inspector-warns.html (accessed 23 June 2013).

Herrnstein, R. and Murray, C. (1994) *The Bell Curve*. New York: Free Press.

HESA (2011) *Statistics – students and qualifiers at UK HE institutions, 2010/11*. Retrieved from www.hesa.ac.uk/content/view/1897/239/ (accessed 7 June 2012).

HM Government (2009) *New Opportunities: Fair chances for the future.* CM 7533. Norwich: The Stationery Office.

— (2010) *Unleashing Aspiration: The government response to the final report of the panel on fair access to the professions.* CM7755. London: The Stationery Office.

— (2011) *Opening Doors, Breaking Barriers: A strategy for social mobility.* London: Cabinet Office.

Hodkinson, P., Sparkes, A. and Hodkinson, H. (1996) *Triumphs and Tears: Young people, markets and the transition from school to work.* London: David Fulton Publishers.

Hoskins, K. (2012a) 'Raising standards 1988 to the present: a new performance policy era?' *Journal of Educational Administration and History,* 44 (1), 5–19.

— (2012b) *Women and Success: Professors in the UK Academy.* Stoke on Trent: Trentham Books.

Jackson, B. and Marsden, D. (1986) *Education and the Working Class.* Originally 1962. London: Ark.

Jackson, M. (2007) 'How far merit selection? Social stratification and the labour market'. *The British Journal of Sociology,* 58 (3), 367–90.

— (2009) 'Disadvantaged through discrimination? The role of employers in social stratification'. *The British Journal of Sociology,* 60 (4), 670–92.

Jensen, A. (1969) 'How much can we boost IQ and scholastic achievement?' *Harvard Educational Review,* 39 (1), 1–123.

Jones, H. (1997) 'Introduction'. In Jones, H. (ed.) *Towards a Classless Society.* London: Routledge, 1–12.

Lambert, P., Prandy, K. and Bottero, W. (2007) 'By slow degrees: two centuries of social reproduction and mobility in Britain'. *Sociological Research Online,* 12 (1). Online. www.socresonline.org.uk/12/1/prandy.html (accessed 11 April 2012).

Lamont, M. and Lareau, A. (1988) 'Cultural capital: allusions, gaps and glissandos in recent theoretical developments'. *Sociological Theory,* 6 (2), 153–68.

Lareau, A. (2002) 'Invisible inequality: social class and childrearing in black families and white families'. *American Sociological Review,* 67 (5), 747–76.

Larner, W. (2000) 'Neo-liberalism: policy, ideology, governmentality'. *Studies in Political Economy,* 63 (Autumn), 5–25.

Levačić, R. and Woods, P. (2002) 'Raising school performance in the league tables (part 1): disentangling the effects of social disadvantage'. *British Educational Research Journal,* 28 (2), 207–26.

Lowe, R. (1997) *Schooling and Social Change 1964–1990.* London: Routledge.

Lupton, R. (2011) '"No change there then!" (?): the onward march of school markets and competition'. *Journal of Educational Administration and History,* 43 (4), 309–23.

Machin, S. (1999) 'Childhood disadvantage and intergenerational transmissions of economic status'. In *Persistent Poverty and Lifetime Inequality: The Evidence.* Proceedings from a workshop of the Centre for Analysis of Social Exclusion, held at HM Treasury, 1998. London: London School of Economics, 17–21. Online. www.discovery.ucl.ac.uk/17030/ (accessed 22 June 2011).

Mahony, P. and Zmroczek, C. (1997) (eds) *Class Matters: 'Working class' women's perspectives on social class.* London: Taylor & Francis.

Major, J. (1995) *Speech at the Queen's Anniversary Prizes Dinner.* Retrieved from www.johnmajor.co.uk/page1067.html (accessed 10 May 2013).

Mansell, W. (2007) *Education by Numbers: The tyranny of testing*. London: Politico's Publishing.

— (2011) 'Improving exam results, but to what end? The limitations of New Labour's control mechanism for schools: assessment-based accountability'. *Journal of Educational Administration and History*, 43 (4), 291–308.

Marshall, G., Swift, A. and Roberts, S. (1997) *Against the Odds? Social class and social justice in industrial societies*. Oxford: Clarendon Press.

Martin, J. (2006) 'Gender and education: change and continuity', in Cole, M. (ed.) *Education, Equality and Human Rights: Issues of gender, 'race', sexuality, disability and social class*. Abingdon: Routledge, 22–42.

Miller, K. (2013) 'We've done awfully well'. *London Review of Books*, 35 (14), 29.

Mills, C. (2008) 'Reproduction and transformation of inequalities in schooling: the transformative potential of the theoretical constructs of Bourdieu'. *British Journal of Sociology of Education*, 29 (1), 79–89.

Mortimore, P. and Whitty, G. (2000) *Can school improvement overcome the effects of disadvantage?* London: University of London, Institute of Education.

Mosley, C. (2003) *Burke's Peerage, Baronetage & Knightage (107th edition)*. Wilmington: Burke's Peerage & Gentry.

NEP (National Equality Panel) (2010) *An Anatomy of Economic Inequality in the UK – Summary*. London: Government Equalities Office.

Nettle, D. (2003) 'Intelligence and class mobility in the British population'. *British Journal of Psychology*, 94, 551–61.

Nunn, A., Johnson, S., Monro, S., Bickerstaffe, T. and Kelsey, S. (2007) *Factors Influencing Social Mobility*. Research Report No. 450, Department for Work and Pensions, Norwich: Stationery Office.

Owen, R. (1969) *A New View of Society and Report to the County of Lanark*. Originally 1813/14. Harmondsworth: Penguin Books.

Paton, G. (2011) 'Education Maintenance Allowance for teenagers cut'. *The Telegraph* 28 March. Online. www.telegraph.co.uk/education/educationnews/8411922/Education-Maintenance-Allowance-for-teenagers-cut.html (accessed 21 June 2011).

— (2012) 'Private school fees "soar at twice the rate of inflation"'. *The Telegraph* 27 August. Online. www.telegraph.co.uk/education/educationnews/9500429/Private-school-fees-soar-at-twice-the-rate-of-inflation.html (accessed 14 April 2013).

Patton, W. and Creed, P. (2007) 'The relationship between career variables and occupational aspirations and expectations for Australian high school adolescents'. *Journal of Career Development*, 34 (2), 127–48.

Payne, G. and Roberts, J. (2002) 'Opening and closing the gates: recent developments in male social mobility in Britain'. *Sociological Research Online*, 6 (4). Online. www.socresonline.org.uk/6/4/payne.html (accessed 11 April 2012).

Perkin, H. (1989) *The Rise of Professional Society*. London: Routledge.

PFAP (The Panel on Fair Access to the Professions) (2009) *Unleashing Aspiration: The final report of the Panel on Fair Access to the Professions*. London: Cabinet Office.

Power, S., Edwards, T., Whitty, G. and Wigfall, V. (2003) *Education and the Middle Class*. Buckingham: Open University Press.

Pring, R. and Walford, G. (1997) *Affirming the comprehensive ideal*. London: Routledge.

Putnam, R. (1995) 'Bowling Alone: America's declining social capital'. *Journal of Democracy,* 6 (1), 65–78. Online. http://xroads.virginia.edu/~HYPER/DETOC/assoc/bowling.html (accessed 11 April 2012).

Raffo, C. (2011) 'Barker's ecology of disadvantage and educational equity: issues of redistribution and recognition'. *Journal of Educational Administration and History,* 43 (4), 325–43.

Reay, D. (2004) '"It's all becoming a habitus": beyond the habitual use of habitus in educational research'. *British Journal of Sociology of Education,* 25 (4), 431–44.

— (2006) 'The zombie stalking English schools: social class and educational inequality'. *British Journal of Educational Studies,* 54 (3), 288–307.

Reay, D., David, E., and Ball, S. (2005) *Degrees of Choice: Social class, race and gender in higher education.* Stoke on Trent: Trentham Books.

Richardson, C. (1977) *Contemporary Social Mobility.* London: Frances Pinter.

Robbins Report (1963) *Report of the Committee appointed by the Prime Minister under the Chairmanship of Lord Robbins.* London: Stationery Office.

Roemer, J. (2000) 'Equality of opportunity'. In Arrow, K., Bowles, S. and Durlauf, S. (eds) *Meritocracy and Economic Inequality.* Princeton: Princeton University Press, 17–32.

Rojewski, J. and Kim, H. (2003) 'Career choice patterns and behavior of work-bound youth during early adolescence'. *Journal of Career Development,* 30 (2), 89–108.

Rutter, M., Maughan, B., Mortimore, P. and Ouston, J. (1979) *Fifteen Thousand Hours: Secondary schools and their effects on children.* London: Open Books.

Sammons, P., Hillman, J. and Mortimore, P. (1995) *Key Characteristics of Effective Schools: A review of school effectiveness research.* London: OFSTED/Institute of Education.

Sanders, D., Korenman, S. and Winship, C. (2000) 'A reanalysis of *The Bell Curve*: intelligence, family background, and schooling'. In Arrow, K., Bowles, S. and Durlauf, S. (eds) *Meritocracy and Economic Inequality.* Princeton: Princeton University Press. 137–78.

Saunders, P. (1995) 'Might Britain be a meritocracy?' *Sociology,* 29 (1), 23–41.

— (2010) *Social Mobility Myths.* London: Civitas.

Savage, M. (2000) *Class Analysis and Social Transformation.* Buckingham: Open University Press.

Scherger, S. and Savage, M. (2010) 'Cultural transmission, educational attainment and social mobility'. *The Sociological Review,* 58 (3), 406–28.

Scott, J. (1996) Comment on Goldthorpe. *British Journal of Sociology,* 47 (3), 507–12.

Sennett, R. and Cobb, J. (1972) *The Hidden Injuries of Class.* New York: Vintage Books.

Sevenoaks School (2012) *Fees.* Retrieved from www.sevenoaksschool.org/fees (accessed 14 July 2013).

Skeggs, B. (1997) *Formations of Class and Gender.* London: Sage.

Skelton, C. and Francis, B. (2009) *Feminism and the Schooling Scandal.* London: Routledge.

SLT (2013) 'Responses to the National Curriculum consultation'. *School Leadership Today*, 5 (1), 11–16. Online. http://library.teachingtimes.com/articles/responsestothenationalcurriculumconsultation.htm (requires subscription) (accessed 5 June 2013).

Smail, D. (2008) *On Deep History and the Brain*. Berkeley: University of California Press.

Smiles, S. (1860) *Self-Help: With illustrations of character and conduct*. London: John Murray.

Smuylan, L. (2004) 'Redefining self and success: becoming teachers and doctors'. *Gender and Education*, 16 (2), 226–45.

South Park Ofsted interim assessment, 2012 – Full reference details withheld to safeguard participant identities.

Stiglitz, J. (2012) *The Price of Inequality: How today's divided society endangers our future*. New York: W.W. Norton.

Strauss, A. and Corbin, J. (1990) *Basics of Qualitative Research: Grounded theory procedures and techniques*. London: Sage.

— (1998) *Basics of Qualitative Research: Techniques and procedures for developing grounded theory* (2nd ed.). Thousand Oaks, CA: Sage.

Swartz, B. (1997) *Culture and Power: The sociology of Pierre Bourdieu*. Chicago: University of Chicago Press.

Tawney, R. (1924) 'Introduction'. In Price, T. *The Story of the Workers' Educational Association from 1903 to 1924*. London: Labour Publishing Company.

Thompson, P. (1997) 'Women, men, and transgenerational family influences in social mobility'. In Bertaux, D. and Thompson, P. (eds) *Pathways to Social Class: a qualitative approach to social mobility*. Oxford: Clarendon Press, 32–61.

Thrupp, M. (1999) *Schools Making A Difference: Let's be realistic*. Buckingham: Open University Press.

Toynbee, P. (2010) 'Tony Blair tried to bury it, but class politics looks set to return'. *The Guardian* 10 July. Online. www.theguardian.com/commentisfree/2010/jul/10/john-prescott-class-politics-old-labour (accessed 21 August 2013).

Vincent, C. (2001) 'Social class and parental agency'. *Journal of Education Policy*, 16 (4), 347–64.

Vincent, C., Ball, S., Rollock, N. and Gillborn, D. (2013) 'Three generations of racism: Black middle-class children and schooling'. *British Journal of Sociology of Education*, 34 (5-6), 929–46.

Vincent, D. (1997) 'Shadow and reality in occupational history: Britain in the first half of the twentieth century'. In Bertaux, D. and Thompson, P. (eds) *Pathways to Social Class: A qualitative approach to social mobility*. Oxford: Clarendon Press, 98–123.

Wallop, H. (2011) 'Youth unemployment hits record'. *The Telegraph* 16 February. Online. www.telegraph.co.uk/finance/economics/8328869/Youth-unemployment-hits-record.html (accessed 21 June 2011).

Webber, R. and Butler, T. (2005) *Classifying Pupils by Where They Live: How well does this predict variations in their GCSE results?* UCL Centre for Advanced Spatial Analysis, Working Paper No. 99. Online. http://discovery.ucl.ac.uk/3277/ (accessed 6 June 2011).

Wilkinson, R. and Pickett, K. (2009) *The Spirit Level: Why equality is better for everyone*. Harmondsworth: Penguin Books.

Williams, M. (1998) 'The social world as knowable'. In Williams, M. and May T. (eds) *Knowing the social world*. Buckingham: Open University Press, 5–21.

Wintour, P. (2004) 'Blair to bank on social mobility'. *The Guardian* 12 October. Online. www.guardian.co.uk/politics/2004/oct/12/socialexclusion.labour (accessed 14 May 2013).

Witz, A. (1997) 'Women and work'. In Robinson, V. and Richardson, D. (eds) *Introducing Women's Studies*. New York: New York University Press, 272–302.

Wright Mills, C. (1970) *The Sociological Imagination*. Harmondsworth: Penguin Books.

Young, M. (1961) *The Rise of the Meritocracy*. Originally 1958. Harmondsworth: Penguin Books.

Index of participants

General index